A Hobbit, a Wardrobe, and a Great War

OTHER BOOKS BY JOSEPH LOCONTE

God, Locke, and Liberty: The Struggle for
Religious Freedom in the West

The Searchers: A Quest for Faith in the Valley of Doubt

The End of Illusions: Religious Leaders
Confront Hitler's Gathering Storm

Seducing the Samaritan: How Government
Contracts Are Reshaping Social Services

A HOBBIT, A WARDROBE, AND A GREAT WAR

*How J. R. R. Tolkien and C. S. Lewis
Rediscovered Faith, Friendship, and
Heroism in the Cataclysm of 1914–1918*

JOSEPH LOCONTE

NELSON
BOOKS
An Imprint of Thomas Nelson

Published in Nashville, Tennessee, by Nelson Books, an imprint of Thomas Nelson. Nelson Books and Thomas Nelson are registered trademarks of HarperCollins Christian Publishing, Inc.

Author is represented by the literary agency of Alive Communications, Inc., 7680 Goddard Street, Suite 200, Colorado Springs, CO 80920, www .alivecommunications.com.

Thomas Nelson titles may be purchased in bulk for educational, business, fund-raising, or sales promotional use. For information, please e-mail SpecialMarkets@ThomasNelson.com.

Library of Congress Control Number: 2015930874

ISBN: 978-0-7180-2176-4
ISBN: 978-0-7180-7923-9 (IE)
ISBN: 978-0-7180-9145-3 (TP)

Printed in the United States of America

24 25 26 27 28 LBC 35 34 33 32 31

For Mom and Dad, who first taught me courage;
for my grandparents, who endured the Great
War; and for the children of Ventotene

"The Great War differed from all ancient wars in the immense power of the combatants and their fearful agencies of destruction, and from all modern wars in the utter ruthlessness with which it was fought. All the horrors of all the ages were brought together, and not only armies but whole populations were thrust into the midst of them."

— Winston Churchill, *The World Crisis, 1911–1918*

"Men whom the trenches cast into intimacy entered into bonds of mutual dependency and sacrifice of self stronger than any of the friendships made in peace and better times. That is the ultimate mystery of the First World War. If we could understand its loves, as well as its hates, we would be nearer to understanding the mystery of human life."

— John Keegan, *The First World War*

"The bravest are surely those who have the clearest vision of what is before them, glory and danger alike, and yet notwithstanding, go out to meet it."

— Thucydides, *History of the Peloponnesian War*

CONTENTS

INTRODUCTION

In the throes of one of the most destructive and dehumanizing wars in world history, something extraordinary occurred, never to be repeated. It happened on Christmas Eve, December 24, 1914.

The "Great War" had been raging for five ferocious months. Neither side could gain a decisive advantage: despite plans and promises to the contrary, the European armies were "racing to deadlock."[1] Deployed into France, most of the original British Expeditionary Force (BEF) of 160,000 men had been wiped out at Mons, Le Cateau, and Ypres. Casualties among the French and German armies were even more staggering. In the opening weeks of the war, the French lost 300,000 men. By the end of December, France and Germany had sustained combat losses of well over 600,000 soldiers, with many more wounded or missing. Some of the fighting had been hand-to-hand. As a German account of the first Battle of Ypres described it: "The enemy fought desperately for every heap of stones and every pile of bricks."[2]

And, yet, on Christmas Eve, the armies on both sides of the Western Front put down their weapons, sang hymns, and treated their enemies as brothers.

No one ordered the now-famous Christmas truce of 1914. No one could have planned for it. It arose spontaneously, without warning, among officers as well as ordinary soldiers, along hundreds of miles of fortified defenses. "Between the trenches, the hated and bitter opponents meet around the Christmas tree and sing Christmas carols," Josef Wenzl, a soldier in the German infantry, wrote to his parents. "This once in a lifetime vision I will not forget."[3]

The biblical Angel of Death descended upon the households of Egypt during Israel's captivity, and destroyed them. This visitation was its reverse: an outbreak of humanity that swept through the lines across the Western Front. Beginning on Christmas Eve and extending into Christmas Day, the killing machines of the Great War went silent. Soldiers came out of their trenches and greeted their adversaries in "No Man's Land," the dead-zone separating enemy defenses. They gathered to sing *"Stille Nacht"* ("Silent Night") and to exchange food, drinks, and tobacco. "Gradually firing ceased almost everywhere along the line that Christmas Eve," writes historian Modris Eksteins. "The Christmas spirit had simply conquered the battlefield."[4]

INTO THE ABYSS

The Christmas spirit of December 1914 was soon dragged into an abyss of death and desolation. Much of the vigor and confidence and decency of the West seemed to vanish with it. Like no other war before it, explains historian John Keegan, the First World War "damaged civilization, the rational and liberal civilization of the European enlightenment, permanently for the worse and, through the damage done, world civilization also."[5] Paul Johnson has described the conflict as "the primal tragedy of modern world civilization, the main reason why the twentieth century turned into such a disastrous epoch for mankind."[6] Winston Churchill, who fought in the war, also reflected somberly on its aftermath: "Injuries were wrought to the structure of human society which a century will not efface, and which may conceivably prove fatal to the present civilization."[7]

The year 2014 marked the centennial of the beginning of that tragedy: the war to make the world safe for democracy, the war to end all wars, the war to usher in the kingdom of heaven. Instead, the Great War laid waste to a continent and destroyed the hopes and lives of a generation. Before it was all over, nearly every family in Europe was grieving the loss of a family member, or helping others to grieve, or caring for a wounded soldier struggling to adjust to civilian life. It was, in the words of author Aldous Huxley, "a gruesome kind of universe."[8]

The livelihoods of hundreds of millions of people, including members of my own family, were disrupted or ruined by the conflict. My paternal grandfather, Michele Loconte, who had emigrated from a small village near Bari, in southern Italy, was living in the United States when hostilities broke out. Drafted into the U.S. Army, he was sent to France in 1918, the year American troops began arriving on the Western Front. He survived the war, but rarely spoke of it. My maternal grandfather, Giuseppe Aiello, left his island home of Ventotene, off the coast of Naples, a region in southern Italy economically decimated during the war years. He arrived in New York City in 1921, just before Mussolini and the fascists swept into power in Rome. Both of my grandparents were determined to start their lives over in the United States.

Scholars continue to debate the causes and outcome of the

war. In *Forgotten Victory*, Gary Sheffield admits the horrific nature of the conflict but insists that "it was neither futile nor meaningless."[9] A belligerent Germany, he writes, had designs for conquest and domination that the democracies of Europe could not ignore. Nevertheless, in Barbara Tuchman's memorable phrase, "the guns of August" signaled the initiation of a European suicide pact: millions of young men would perish in the trenches and the barbed wire and the mechanized slaughter of a conflict that no one had imagined and no one knew how to stop.

Like no other force in history, the First World War permanently altered the political and cultural landscape of Europe, America, and the West. In the judgment of more than one historian, the war became "the axis on which the modern world turned."[10] Literary critic Roger Sale has called the conflict "the single event most responsible for shaping the modern idea that heroism is dead."[11] For a generation of men and women, it brought the end of innocence—and the end of faith.

AGAINST THE TIDE

Yet for two extraordinary authors and friends, J. R. R. Tolkien and C. S. Lewis, the Great War deepened their spiritual quest. Both men served as soldiers on the Western Front, survived the trenches, and used the experience of that conflict to shape their Christian imagination. Tolkien created *The Hobbit* and then *The Lord of the Rings*, the second best-selling novel ever written and among the most influential books of the twentieth century. Lewis earned fame for *The Chronicles of Narnia*, a series of seven immensely popular children's books ranked among the classics. It can be argued that these epic tales—involving the sorrows and triumphs of war—would never have been written had these authors not been flung into the crucible of combat.

The First World War placed an immense burden of loss on their generation. "Battles are won by slaughter and manoeuver," Churchill once observed. "The greater the general, the more he contributes to manoeuver, the less he demands in slaughter."[12] The generals of this war demanded much in slaughter. By the time of the Armistice, more than nine million soldiers lay dead and roughly thirty-seven million wounded. On average, there were about 6,046 men killed every day of the war, a war that lasted 1,566 days. In Great Britain, almost six million men—a quarter of Britain's adult male population—passed through the ranks of the army. About one in eight perished.[13]

Tolkien and Lewis might easily have been among their number. As a second lieutenant in the BEF, Tolkien spent many days and nights on the Western Front, often under fire. He fought at the Battle of the Somme, one of the fiercest concentrations of killing in the history of human conflict. "One has indeed personally to come under the shadow of war to feel full its oppression," Tolkien wrote decades later. "But as the years go by it seems now often forgotten that to be caught in youth by 1914 was no less hideous an experience than to be involved in 1939 and the following years. By 1918 all but one of my close friends were dead."[14]

Also commissioned as a second lieutenant in the BEF, Lewis was sent immediately to the front. The experience of six months of trench warfare, a vortex of suffering and death, remained with him throughout his life. As he once reflected, unromantically: "My memories of the last war haunted my dreams for years. Military service, to be plain, includes the threat of every temporal evil."[15] Lewis would describe the emotion of grief as "the steady barrage on a trench in World War One, hours of it with no let-up for a moment."[16] Like Tolkien, he lost most of his closest friends in the conflict.

After the war, Tolkien and Lewis made their way to Oxford University, where they took up their vocations as instructors in English literature. They met for the first time in 1926, and a bond of friendship was established that would transform their lives and careers. Tolkien would play a crucial role in Lewis's conversion to Christianity, while Lewis would be the decisive voice in persuading Tolkien to complete *The Hobbit* and *The Lord of the Rings*. Given the massive and enduring influence of their works, it is hard to think of a more consequential friendship in the twentieth century—a friendship that emerged from the suffering and sorrow of a world war.

These Christian authors were swimming against the tide of their times. During the postwar years, many veterans composed fiercely anti-war novels and poetry. Many more became moral cynics. Yet Tolkien and Lewis—deeply aware of "the beauty and mortality of the world"—insisted that war could inspire noble sacrifice for humane purposes.[17] As a generation of young writers rejected faith in the God of the Bible, they produced stories imbued with the themes of guilt and grace, sorrow and consolation.

Journalist Walter Lipmann, reflecting on the spiritual consequences of the First World War, lamented that "trivial illusions" had displaced traditional religious belief. "What most distinguishes the generation who have approached maturity since the debacle of idealism at the end of the War is not their rebellion against the religion and the moral code of their parents," he wrote, "but their disillusionment with their own rebellion."[18] Part of the achievement of Tolkien and Lewis was to reintroduce into the popular imagination a Christian vision of hope in a world tortured by doubt and disillusionment.

A FLIGHT BACK TO REALITY

Both authors, of course, have been accused of escapism. Their choice of literary genre, the romantic myth, was by some estimations "essentially an attempt to liberate themselves from the ugliness and moral impasse of the modern world."[19] Yet neither Tolkien nor Lewis took their cues from works extolling escapist fantasies or the glorification of war. Tolkien was drawn to tales such as *Beowulf*, with its dark view of the contest between good and evil. "Its characteristic struggle between man and monster must end ultimately, within Time, in man's defeat," writes literature professor Patricia Meyer Spacks. "Yet man continues to struggle; his weapons are the hobbit-weapons: naked will and courage."[20] Thus in *The Lord of the Rings* we find great sobriety about the prospects of final victory in this present life, as in the words of Galadriel: "Through the ages of the world we have fought the long defeat."

When Lewis was asked to name the books that did the most to shape his professional life, he included Virgil's *Aeneid*, the mythic and violent story of Rome's beginnings. It is no nursery school fairy tale. Aeneas's subordination of desire to duty, his willingness to accept his arduous calling, makes him a heroic figure. But, as Lewis once observed, the travails he must endure make the work a "great and hard and bitter epic."[21] Though written for children, the same might be said of Lewis's *The Chronicles of Narnia*. There is an ultimate triumph of light over darkness in the story, but not without bloodshed, terrible loss, and the fear of death. "Take my advice," says Mr. Beaver, "whenever you meet anything that's going to be human and isn't yet, or used to be human once and isn't now, or ought to be human and isn't, you keep your eyes on it and feel for your hatchet."[22]

Tolkien and Lewis were attracted to the genres of myth and romance not because they sought to escape the world, but because for them the real world had a mythic and heroic quality. The world is the setting for great conflicts and great quests: it creates scenes of remorseless violence, grief, and suffering, as well as deep compassion, courage, and selfless sacrifice. In an era that exalted cynicism and irony, Tolkien and Lewis sought to reclaim an older tradition of the epic hero. Their depictions of the struggles of Middle-earth and Narnia do not represent a flight from reality, but rather a return to a more realistic view of the world as we actually find it.

Indeed, it was the experience of war that provided much of the raw material for the characters and themes of their imaginative works. In a talk called "Learning in War Time," Lewis explained how war exposes the folly of placing our happiness in utopian schemes to transform society. "If we thought we were building up a heaven on earth, if we looked for something that would turn the present world from a place of pilgrimage into a permanent city satisfying the soul of man, we are disillusioned, and not a moment too soon."[23] As we'll see, unlike the disillusionment that overwhelmed much of his generation, Lewis would use the experience of war—its horror as well as its nobility—as a guidepost to moral clarity.

Likewise for Tolkien, who emerged from the war with a profound respect for the ordinary soldier. As an officer in the British army, he could not befriend the many privates who made up his battalion, nor the "batmen," the servants assigned to look after an officer's gear and attend to his daily needs. But war has a way of softening military hierarchies. As Tolkien fought alongside these soldiers, he witnessed again and again their remarkable determination under fire. Indeed, as he later acknowledged, one of the great heroic figures in *The Lord of the Rings* is based on his firsthand knowledge of the men in the trenches of the Great War: "My 'Sam Gamgee' is indeed a reflection of the English soldier, of the privates and batmen I knew in the 1914 war, and recognized as so far superior to myself."[24]

A MESSAGE FOR OUR TIME

Military historian Victor Davis Hanson once observed that the history of the West is almost the history of warfare. "Democratic citizenship," he writes, "requires knowledge of war."[25] Tolkien and Lewis never sought the intimate knowledge of combat that they acquired as young men. Indeed, it cannot be emphasized enough that neither man welcomed the arrival of war or ever romanticized what war was about. "I am no warrior at all," protests Pippin in *The Lord of the Rings*, "and dislike any thought of battle."[26] How could it be otherwise, given what they and their generation endured?

Nevertheless, the Great War helped to frame the sensibilities of both authors, a fact that seems neglected by scholars and ordinary admirers alike. In the centennial year of the beginning of the First World War, publishing houses began stirring up interest again in the conflict. Historians tend to focus on the outbreak of the war, the tactics of the generals, the all-out destruction, or the embittered memoirs and novels that appeared in its wake. Most of the newest offerings examine the war from nearly every angle—military, political, social, economic—except from the vantage point of faith. What is needed, however, is a fresh appraisal of the spiritual calamity of the war and the human condition in light of this experience.

The story of the war's impact on the creative outlook of Tolkien and Lewis can help historians better understand its moral and spiritual consequences for an entire generation. Conversely, admirers of their fiction can benefit immensely from a deeper appreciation of the chastening experience of war. Believers and skeptics alike may be surprised to learn how two of the most celebrated writers of the twentieth century responded to the Great War: how they deployed their Christian conscience to challenge a prevailing culture of postwar grief, gloom, and unbelief.

Their achievement, and its importance in our own day, should not be undervalued. Some authors see in their work "despair over modern social and political life" and "deep pessimism about life and society."[27] But such a critique seems impoverished by its own gloomy assumptions. Tolkien and Lewis offer an understanding of the human story that is both tragic and hopeful: they suggest that war is a symptom of the ruin and wreckage of human life, but that it points the way to a life restored and transformed by grace.

In this sense, they offer a challenge to those who view war as a ready solution to our problems as well as those who condemn any war as an unqualified evil. Neither Tolkien nor Lewis fell prey to the extreme reactions to the war so typical of their era. "We know from the experience of the last twenty years," wrote Lewis in 1944, "that a terrified and angry pacifism is one of the roads that lead to war."[28] Tolkien decried "the utter stupid waste of war," yet admitted "it will be necessary to face it in an evil world."[29] Their recourse was to draw us back to the heroic tradition: a mode of thought tempered by the realities of combat and fortified by belief in a God of justice and mercy.

Perhaps the character of Faramir, the Captain of Gondor in *The Lord of the Rings*, expresses it best.[30] He possesses humility as well as great courage—a warrior with a "grave tenderness in his eyes"—who takes no delight in the prospect of battle. As such, he conveys a message that bears repeating at the present moment, in a world that is no stranger to the sorrows and ravages of war. "War must be, while we defend our lives against a destroyer who would devour all," he explains. "But I do not love the bright sword for its sharpness, nor the arrow for its swiftness, nor the warrior for his glory. I love only that which they defend."[31]

CHAPTER 1

THE FUNERAL OF A GREAT MYTH

On May 13, 1901, three months after joining Parliament, twenty-six-year-old Winston Churchill rises to deliver a rebuke to his Conservative Party colleagues in the House of Commons. Anxious about German designs in Europe, some British politicians are demanding that the government develop an army capable of defeating a European foe. Such a war, most believe, would be limited and decisive—and immensely beneficial to the victor.

But Churchill has racked up battle experiences in India, the Sudan, and the Boer War in South Africa. He realizes that the nature of warfare is changing; a conflict in Europe would be nothing like the colonial wars of the previous century, which were fought by small professional armies against ill-equipped foes, and brought to a swift conclusion. "I have frequently been astonished to hear with what composure and how glibly Members, and even Ministers, talk of a European war," he says. Such a conflict, he warns, would end "in the ruin of the vanquished and the scarcely less fatal commercial dislocation and exhaustion of the conquerors."[1] It would not be the last time Churchill found himself out of step with conventional political wisdom.

By the start of the twentieth century, attitudes about war and what it could accomplish were bound up with a singular, overarching idea. Let's call it "The Myth of Progress." Perhaps the most widely held view in the years leading up to the Great War was that Western civilization was marching inexorably forward, that humanity itself was maturing, evolving, advancing—that new vistas of political, cultural, and spiritual achievement were within reach. The Renaissance message of Pico della Mirandola, *Oration on the Dignity of Man* (1486), in which the Creator extols mankind's fearsome possibilities, fairly captures the mood: "We have made you a creature neither mortal nor immortal, in order that you may, as the free and proud shaper of your own being, fashion yourself in the form you may prefer. It will be in your power to descend to the lower, brutish forms of life; you will be able, through your own decision, to rise again to the superior orders whose life is divine."[2]

The thinkers and writers who informed the generation of J. R. R. Tolkien and C. S. Lewis were certain which direction mankind was headed. Their confidence in human progress led many to believe that, with the help of modern technologies, wars could be fought and won with minimal cost in life and treasure.

The argument is straightforward: Rational Europeans would no longer indulge in the kind of extended and brutal campaigns of previous years. The days of religious wars, the Napoleonic Wars, the Crimean War—these were relics of a bygone era. Short, tidy wars would be the norm, with healthy economic and political outcomes. "The concept of states waging war to the point of absolute exhaustion," concluded a German author in 1908, "is beyond the European cultural experience."[3] A few years before the outbreak of World War I, when Germany was agitating for a confrontation with Britain and France over a port on the Moroccan coast, an anti-war leader in the German Parliament was shouted down with these words: "After every war things are better!"[4]

The belief in progress led others to argue that the West would soon dispense with war altogether as the remnant of a primitive, unenlightened epoch. British writer Norman Angell, in his book *The Great Illusion*, explained that the great democracies of Europe were coming to realize that war would produce severe economic hardship and losses, and would take all measures necessary to avoid it.

According to Angell, the Industrial Revolution—by establishing a pattern of economic growth and interdependence—had changed the dynamic among nation-states. The great industrial nations of Britain, France, Germany, and the United States were "losing the psychological impulse to war," he wrote, just as they abandoned the impulse to kill their neighbors over religion. "The least informed of us realizes that the whole trend of history is against the tendency for men to attack the ideals and the beliefs of other men."[5] In the new age of international commerce and communication, nations would naturally devote infinitely more resources to peaceful endeavors than to preparations for war. "How can we possibly expect to keep alive warlike qualities," he asked, "when all our interests and activities—all our environments, in short—are peace-like?"[6]

First published in 1909, *The Great Illusion* became a run-away bestseller. It was translated into French, German, Italian, and Russian, and within a few years went through more than ten printings in English. The book seemed to speak to a deep and widely shared aspiration: the "perpetual peace" imagined by philosophers such as Immanuel Kant. Science fiction writer H. G. Wells recalled the mood: "I think that in the decades before 1914 not only I but most of my generation—in the British Empire, America, France and indeed throughout most of the civilized world—thought that war was dying out. So it seemed to us."[7]

It is a view that was especially congenial to religious leaders, even on the eve of the conflict. Britain's National Peace Council, a coalition of religious and secular peace organizations, foresaw a new era of international harmony. The 1914 edition of its *Peace Yearbook* offers this astonishing prediction:

> Peace, the babe of the nineteenth century, is the strong youth of the twentieth century; for War, the product of anarchy and fear, is passing away under the growing and persistent pressure of world organization, economic necessity, human intercourse, and that change of spirit, that social sense and newer aspect of worldwide life which is the insistent note, the *Zeitgeist* of the age.[8]

This "change of spirit," this faith in progress that would render war an anachronism, had found a champion in Victorian England. In the waning years of the nineteenth century—the decade into which both Tolkien and Lewis were born—Great Britain was at the apex of its political, economic, and cultural achievements. Its parliamentary democracy was the oldest and most stable in all of Europe, its colonial holdings were the largest, it controlled a quarter of the planet's land surface, and its Navy ruled the seas. In short, the British crown reigned over the most extensive empire in world history.[9] Despite its imperialist excesses, argues historian Niall Ferguson, "no organization has done more to impose Western norms of law, order and governance around the world."[10] Tolkien and Lewis were part of a generation of Britons who equated their nation's growth and prosperity with the progress of civilization itself.

THE PROMISE OF THE CRYSTAL PALACE

And why wouldn't they? As the leader of the Industrial Revolution, England had pioneered the technological advances that were sweeping Europe. Its dominance was unquestioned at the first World's Fair, held in London in 1851, "at the zenith of Britain's imperial pomp."[11] An enormous glass and cast-iron monument was built to house the Great Exhibition. Known as the Crystal Palace, it was the largest glass structure in the world and a symbol of Victorian England's cultural triumphs. On display were roughly one hundred thousand exhibits, spread across ten miles of floor space, and grouped into four main categories: raw materials, machinery, manufacturers, and fine arts. Of the fifteen thousand contributors, Britain claimed half the display space. Queen Victoria declared the opening day of the fair "the greatest day in our history."

Even greater days seemed to lie ahead. Railway engines, steam engines, blast furnaces, textile plants, coal and iron mines were turning nature into the handmaiden of humanity.

As historian Roger Osborne explains, science-based technology was improving life for ordinary people, making it easier and safer. And healthier: the principles of science were producing better sanitation and living conditions, and enabling new strides in medicine and the treatment of diseases. The new technologies, the explosive growth of cities, the productivity of industry—all these forces were changing the physical nature of European life.[12]

It was this encroachment of technological life into rural England that Tolkien came to resent. Born in 1892, John Ronald Reuel Tolkien developed a deep attachment to his home in West Midlands, a county that was already a mix of rural countryside and urban development. Tolkien spent his early years in "a pre-mechanical age," and regarded growing up around Birmingham—a hub of the Industrial Revolution—as one of the "really significant" facts of his youth. Today, West Midlands is one of the most heavily urbanized counties in Great Britain.

"How real, how startlingly alive is a factory chimney compared with an elm tree," Tolkien wrote scornfully. "Poor obsolete thing, insubstantial dream of an escapist!"[13] Tolkien's love of the English countryside, his attachment to nature, rebelled against the chaotic industrialization of his day. His dissent found an imaginative outlet: the bucolic world of the hobbits, the region of Middle-earth known as the Shire.

Biographer Humphrey Carpenter believes that the mechanized disruption of the world Tolkien loved "defined the nature of his scholarly work," motivating him to create the Shire and its homely inhabitants.[14] As Tolkien once told his publisher, the Shire "is based on rural England and not any other country in the world."[15] The house of his famous hobbit, Bilbo Baggins, takes its name—"Bag End"—from his aunt's farm in Worcestershire. "I am in fact a Hobbit (in all but size)," he admitted. "I like gardens, trees and unmechanized farmlands; I smoke a pipe, and like good plain food (unrefrigerated), but detest French cooking."[16]

In contrast, Tolkien viewed the overreliance on technology, "the Machine," as a step toward dominating others. The act of "bulldozing the real world," Tolkien wrote, involves "coercing other wills."[17] Hence, the hateful realm of Mordor is sustained by its black engines and factories, which Sauron introduces as his forces invade the Shire. This theme would absorb Tolkien for much of his career.

Writing in the 1940s, Tolkien lamented "the tragedy and despair of all machinery laid bare." The tragedy, as he saw it, was the attempt to use technology to actualize our desires and increase our power over the world around us—all of which leaves us unsatisfied. Tolkien attached a spiritual significance to the problem: "And in addition to this fundamental disability of a creature, is added the Fall, which makes our devices not only fail of their desire but turn to new and horrible evil."[18] It surely was this view that caused him, in *The Lord of the Rings*, to portray the enemies of nature in the darkest of terms. Saruman the Wizard "has a mind of metal and wheels; and he does not care for growing things, except as far as they serve him for the moment," he wrote. "And now it is clear that he is a black traitor."[19]

Clive Staples Lewis was born in 1898, just outside Belfast in Northern Ireland. The family moved to Little Lea, on the edge of suburbia, a town surrounded by green hills. From his house he could watch ships of all kinds navigate in and out of Belfast Lough. "The sound of a steamer's horn at night," he wrote, "still conjures up my whole boyhood."[20] Within a mile of his home was "indisputably open hilly farmland," which Lewis and his brother Warren explored by bicycle.[21]

Lewis became as dubious as Tolkien of the promises of industrialization to uplift the human condition, a skepticism that he would carry throughout his life. "Near here they are about to demolish part of a lovely beechwood in order to straighten the main London Rd, drat them," he wrote a week before his death in November 1963. "There are times when I wonder if the invention of the internal combustion engine was not an even greater disaster than that of the hydrogen bomb!" Modern assumptions about "progress" that disregard the rhythms and traditions of the past will come under attack. "I care more how humanity lives than how long," he wrote. "Progress, for me, means increasing the goodness and happiness of individual lives. For the species, as for each man, mere longevity seems to me a contemptible idea."[22]

It is a conviction that appears often in his writing, where he lampoons the growth of technologies and bureaucracies at the expense of human freedom. In *The Voyage of the Dawn Treader*, King Caspian tangles with slave traders who, with statistics and graphs, try to justify their operations as "economic development." Caspian wants the trade ended:

> "But that would be putting the clock back," gasped the governor. "Have you no idea of progress, of development?"
>
> "I have seen both in an egg," said Caspian. "We call it 'Going Bad' in Narnia. This trade must stop."[23]

Both authors regarded twentieth-century modernization as a threat to human societies because they viewed the natural world as the handiwork of God and thus integral to human happiness. As such, nature was an essential ally in the struggle against these dehumanizing forces.

In the climactic battles for Narnia and Middle-earth, Nature herself joins in the war against tyranny. Tolkien's walking, humanoid trees, the Ents, are among the most memorable figures in his stories. Led by Treebeard—the oldest living creature in Middle-earth—the Ents were created to guard the forest from orcs and other deadly forces. The calamitous War of the Elves and Sauron, fought in the Second Age, decimated the land, forcing the Ents to confine themselves to Fangorn Forest.

Though hoping to avoid the War of the Ring, Treebeard and his companions can no longer tolerate the atrocities committed against them and the forest. As the wizard Gandalf explains, they finally decide to march against Saruman—"the last march of the Ents"—and play a decisive role in his defeat. "But now his long slow wrath is brimming over, and all the forest is filled with it . . . its tide is turned against Saruman and the axes of Isengard. A thing is about to happen which has not happened since the Elder Days: the Ents are going to wake up and find that they are strong."[24]

Lewis likewise viewed nature as an intrinsic part of human life. This is why the Narnia novels give such a prominent role to its animals. Even the smallest of creatures—Reepicheep the mouse, for example—can display the greatest of human virtues. As biographer Alister McGrath writes, Lewis understood humanity's relationship with animals, and with the rest of the natural world, as potentially ennobling and fulfilling. "Lewis's portrayal of animal characters in Narnia is partly a protest against shallow assertions of humanity's right to do what it pleases with nature."[25]

In *Prince Caspian*, the character Trufflehunter explains to Caspian why it will be difficult to wake the spirits of the trees in the battle against Miraz, the unlawful king of Narnia, and his Telmarine army: "We have no power over them. Since the Humans came into the land, felling forests and defiling streams, the Dryads and Naiads have sunk into deep sleep."[26] Nevertheless, the war cannot be won without their help, and Aslan summons them to join the crusade: the "woods on the move." In a scene reminiscent of the "last march of the Ents," trees from every direction converge like stormy waves upon the battlefield: "But soon neither their cries nor the sound of weapons could be heard any more, for both were drowned in the ocean-like roar of the Awakened Trees as they plunged through the ranks of Peter's army, and then on, in pursuit of the Telmarines."[27]

It is Nature's revenge against Man: the industrialized exploitation of the physical world cannot go unpunished. This judgment against man's assault on his environment could only have been deepened by the experience of the Great War. Never before in the history of warfare had technology wrought such physical devastation: an industrialized holocaust as terrifying in its effects on nature as on men. What a regimental historian said of the Battle of the Somme could be applied to many of the battles from 1914–18 that defaced the European landscape: "In that field of fire nothing could live."[28] Writing three years after the conclusion of the war, author Vera Brittain described the scene near Amiens, as she drove to find the grave of her fiancé. She witnessed "a series of shell-racked roads between the grotesque trunks of skeleton trees, with their stripped, shattered branches still pointing to heaven in grim protest against man's ruthless cruelty to nature as well as man."[29]

THE MASTERY OF NATURE
WITHOUT GOD

As we'll see, Tolkien and Lewis imported these images, sometimes quite directly, into their works of fiction—a quiet protest against the march of progress. Nevertheless, by the time they entered adulthood, the preindustrial past had given way to a present enthralled with science and technology. "Between 1900 and 1914, technological, social, and political advances swept Europe and America on a scale unknown in any such previous timespan," writes historian Max Hastings, "the blink of an eye in human experience."[30]

Just consider the breakthroughs that appear at the turn of the century. In 1900, as if to symbolize man's evolutionary ascent, Charles Seeberger invents the first modern escalator. The next year, Marconi delivers the first transatlantic radio signal, while Hubert Booth invents a compact vacuum cleaner. In 1902 there appear the first air conditioner, lie detector, and neon light. In 1903 the Wright brothers successfully test the first gas-motored and manned airplane; the first steam turbine generator appears the same year. In 1904 the tractor is invented. In 1905 Albert Einstein stuns the scientific community with his theory of relativity. Sonar is developed in 1906 and the first air-conditioned hospital appears in Boston. In 1907 color photography is invented. In 1908 Henry Ford produces 10,660 Model T automobiles in his assembly line, making cars affordable for large numbers of people. Instant coffee is invented in 1909 (modern-day coffee snobs view this as a sign of the *decline* of the West). In 1910 Thomas Edison unveils the first talking motion picture, while physicist Marie Curie successfully isolates radium, a feat that will make her the first woman to receive the Nobel Prize.

All this self-generated progress, this mastery of nature, was occurring without the help of religion. For many Europeans and Americans, Christianity seemed irrelevant to the insights and blessings of the new technologies. "Using his own natural intelligence, and without the aid of Holy Scripture's divine revelation, man had penetrated nature's mysteries, transformed his universe, and immeasurably enhanced his existence," writes cultural historian Richard Tarnas in *The Passion of the Western Mind*. "Man was responsible for his own earthly destiny. His own wits and will could change his world. Science gave man a new faith—not only in scientific knowledge, but in himself."[31]

The newfound faith in humanity, however, did not imply contentment with man's place in nature. Many began to wonder if the same scientific principles that were so drastically transforming the physical world might be used to improve its most important inhabitants: the human species. If science could be so effective at probing and improving the natural world, couldn't it do the same for human society?[32]

Thus, it was not only technological innovations that were emboldening the believers in progress. Scientists and social thinkers were also transforming the way Europeans and Americans viewed human nature and the cosmos. Charles Darwin, of course, paved the way with his theory of evolution. Darwin's *On the Origin of Species* (1859) seemed to explain scientifically, for the first time, how organisms change, adapt, and become more complex. It was intended as a theory of biology.

Yet Darwin himself suggested that the idea of natural selection, the struggle for existence of the most fit and capable, might be extended to other areas. Thanks to Herbert Spencer, a British social theorist, Darwin's theory was reinterpreted as a doctrine of unremitting progress—and applied to society at large. Every realm of human endeavor, from politics to economics to ethics, fell under its refining influence. Humankind, Spencer wrote, was in a long process of adaption and self-improvement: "And the belief in human perfectibility merely amounts to the belief that, in virtue of this process, man will eventually become completely suited to his mode of life."[33]

The impact of Spencer on Anglo-American thought can hardly be exaggerated. In the decades leading up to the First World War, it was virtually impossible to undertake any intellectual work without mastering Spencer.[34] His "towering influence" would have been inconceivable had he not arisen in an age of steel and steam engines, competition, exploitation, and struggle.[35] US Supreme Court Justice Oliver Wendell Holmes doubted that "any writer of English except Darwin has done so much to affect our whole way of thinking about the universe."[36]

Thus, Spencer's social interpretation of Darwinian science energized the most powerful narrative at the beginning of the twentieth century. The Myth of Progress was not just one story among many. It was *the* story, the metanarrative of all the stories about our mortal lives, a comprehensive explanation of the meaning of human existence.

The Myth of Progress was proclaimed from nearly every sector of society. Scientists, physicians, educators, industrialists, salesmen, politicians, preachers—they all agreed on the upward flight of humankind. Each breakthrough in medicine, science, and technology seemed to confirm the Myth. Every invention and innovation was offered up as evidence: whether it was Marconi's radio messages or the Maxim machine gun, such advances were ordained by the gods of progress.[37] Thus, what began as a theory about biological *change* ripened into an assumption—a dogma—about human *improvement*, even perfection.

Or so it seemed to C. S. Lewis and many of his generation. "I grew up believing in this Myth and I have felt—I still feel—its almost perfect grandeur," he wrote. "To those brought up on the Myth nothing seems more normal, more natural, more plausible, than that chaos should turn into order, death into life, ignorance into knowledge. It is one of the most moving and satisfying world dramas which have ever been imagined."[38]

The Myth of Progress proves to be irresistible, especially to those repelled by traditional Christianity and its unpleasant doctrines of guilt, judgment, and repentance. Indeed, the triumph of science and technology seemed to leave no meaningful role for religion or the supernatural. Science, not religion, was driving human achievement. Its new dominance left many believers struggling for resources with which to shore up the credibility of their faith. "Looked at with the cold eye of empiricism," writes historian James Turner, Christianity's claims to knowledge about the cosmos "stood naked as a babe."[39]

By the end of the nineteenth century, theologians and social reformers were frantically recasting Christianity as a "social gospel" of human advancement, perfectly in step with the *zeitgeist*. Although many of these efforts were laudable in their intent—programs to alleviate poverty, provide for orphans, reduce alcoholism, improve working conditions—they, too, got swept up in the Myth. Pastors such as Lyman Abbott, author of *The Evolution of Christianity*, predicted steady moral development: "There is a God in history, as there is a God in nature—a God who is working out some great design among men, as there is a God who is working out great designs through all material and mechanical phenomena."[40] The Christian religion, declared social gospel leader Washington Gladden, "must be a religion less concerned about getting men to heaven than about fitting them for their proper work on the earth."[41]

THE GOSPEL OF EUGENICS

In an age of technological triumphalism, "fitting" people for their "proper work" in the world meant applying scientific methods to improve the species. In a word: *eugenics.* Coined by Francis Galton, a cousin of Darwin, the word comes from the Greek, meaning "good birth."

Speaking to a learned society in London in 1909, Galton explained how the tools of evolutionary science could be used to better the human race. "What Nature does blindly, slowly, ruthlessly, man may do providently, quickly, and kindly," he said. "As it lies within his power, so it becomes his duty to work in that direction."[42] Armed with statistical research documenting Britain's genetic decline, Galton envisioned a massive societal investment in eugenics programs. "If a twentieth part of the cost and pains were spent in measures for the improvement of the human race that is spent on the improvement of the breed of horses and cattle, what a galaxy of genius might we not create!" he said. "We might introduce prophets and high priests of civilization into the world, as surely as we can propagate idiots by mating cretins."[43]

Galton's gospel of eugenics found fertile soil in Britain, in the intellectual salons of Europe, and in the United States. Beginning in the early years of the twentieth century, eugenics scientists called for programs to manipulate human reproduction. They advocated for laws to segregate the so-called feebleminded into state colonies, to live out their lives in celibacy. They led the drive to restrict immigration from countries whose citizens might pollute their national gene pools. And they supported sterilization laws aimed at men and women whose "germplasm" threatened the eugenic vitality of the nation.[44]

In Britain, the Eugenics Education Society was founded in 1907 to take up the cause. By 1913, the American Genetic Association was established in the United States to promote the doctrines of racial purity. Eugenics became an academic discipline at many colleges and universities. Beginning in 1912, a series of International Eugenics Conferences were held in London and New York, creating a global venue for eugenicists and their supporters. "It [eugenics] must be introduced into the national conscience, like a new religion," Galton explained. "It has, indeed, strong claims to become an orthodox religious tenet of the future, for Eugenics cooperates with the workings of Nature by securing that humanity shall be represented by the fittest races."[45]

Religious leaders, especially those in the liberal wing of the Christian church, would answer the call. Ministers in the Church of England held a Church Congress in 1910 in Cambridge, inviting several members of the Royal Commission on the Feeble-Minded to participate. Attendees that day were treated to "brilliant" addresses urging the clergy to promote the eugenics agenda at every turn. The National Church had "a very great responsibility towards the race," according to one speaker, and "the future belongs to those nations whose religious leaders realize this responsibility." An American observer at the Congress concluded, with apparent envy, that the Church of England "was ready, in matters of social action, to 'think biologically.' "[46]

Two years later in London, the Anglican bishops of Birmingham, Oxford, and Ripon were among the vice presidents of the First International Eugenics Congress. Major Leonard Darwin, the son of Charles Darwin, was the presiding officer—illustrating the intellectual bond between Darwinism and eugenics. That same year, the influential Protestant minister F. B. Meyer, author of *Religion and Race-Regeneration* (1912), warned that the high birthrates of Catholics, Jews, and the feebleminded presented a collective menace to society.[47]

For Tolkien and Lewis, all of this represented a frontal assault on human dignity: a reduction of the individual to mere biology. In their imaginative works they invariably depict their characters as physical *and* spiritual beings, responsible for their souls even as they are constrained by their earthly nature. Their fictional worlds are filled with nonhuman races—elves, dwarves, hobbits, centaurs, etc.—who nonetheless all share this fundamental attribute. For each of them, virtue and corruption are equally plausible.[48] As Tolkien insisted, even the dreadful orcs are presented as rational beings, "though horribly corrupted, if no more so than many Men to be met today."[49]

This helps to explain the bitter conflict between the forces of slavery and liberty that runs through their stories: no creatures are born for captivity, and none have a birthright to oppress others. In *The Lord of the Rings*, the followers of Sauron, the Dark Lord, serve him out of fear; they are no more than slaves in his realm. Thus we see the use of genetic engineering—the creation of robotic orcs—to extend the dictatorship of Mordor throughout the world. At its heart, the War of the Ring is a struggle to preserve the essential freedom and humanity of the inhabitants of Middle-earth. "It would be a grievous blow to the world," says

Gandalf the Grey, "if the Dark Power overcame the Shire; if all your kind . . . became enslaved."[50]

For his part, Lewis warned against the bondage imposed upon humanity when, under the guise of scientific progress, men and women are regarded as "patients." In *Perelandra*, the second in his *Space Trilogy*, we meet Professor Weston, a famous physicist and devotee of the new science. Weston is an advocate of "emergent evolution," a process by which the human species is "thrusting its way upward and ever upward" toward new heights of achievement. He boasts that his new beliefs have swept away all his old conceptions of our moral obligations to others. "Man in himself is nothing," he explains. "The forward movement of Life—the growing spirituality—is everything."[51] Weston emerges as an essentially satanic figure.

For both authors the "conquest of Nature" would prove catastrophic. In the name of progress, a handful of elites would dominate the lives and destinies of millions. As Tolkien wrote in *Mythopoeia*: "I will not walk with your progressive apes / erect and sapient. Before them gapes / the dark abyss to which their progress tends."[52] Likewise, Lewis warned that the final stage of this process would arrive when human beings achieved full mastery over themselves. Eugenics, prenatal conditioning, education, and psychology would all play a part in "the abolition of man," the surrender of our essential humanity. "For the power of Man to make himself what he pleases means, as we have seen, the power of some men to make other men what they please."[53]

Bizarre as it may seem, the "scientific" manipulation of human beings, all under the banner of progress, became the consensus view of the academic communities in England, Germany, and the United States, just as Tolkien and Lewis were launching their careers. Serious efforts were underway to identify biological "defectives" so they could be incarcerated and sterilized. Marriage laws were seen as ineffective, while immigration restrictions couldn't stop defective people who were already here from procreating. Incredibly, *forced sterilization*—considered cheap, safe, and permanent—became the stated goal of the eugenics movement. Beginning in 1907, states such as Indiana passed sterilization laws "to prevent procreation of confirmed criminals, idiots, imbeciles and rapists." The United States acquired the noxious distinction of being the first nation in the West to legalize compulsory sterilization.[54]

Catholics and conservative Protestants resisted these laws, but the eugenic tide appeared to be turning against them. By the 1920s, hundreds of American churches participated in a national "eugenics sermon contest." As the Rev. Kenneth McArthur, a winner from Sterling, Massachusetts, put it in his sermon: "If we take seriously the Christian purpose of realizing on earth the ideal divine society, we shall welcome every help which science affords."[55] Oliver Wendell Holmes was an apostle for the new science, having authored the 1927 Supreme Court opinion upholding Virginia's sterilization law. "It is better for all the world, if instead of waiting to execute degenerate offspring for crime, or to let them starve for their imbecility, society can prevent those who are manifestly unfit from continuing their kind," he wrote. "Three generations of imbeciles are enough."[56]

THE HUMAN PREDICAMENT

Here, on shameless display, is the crisis of faith at the start of the twentieth century. Historians tend to interpret Darwin's influence as the essential solvent that destroyed belief in God: the laws of natural selection required no Law-Giver. Thus, evolution made God redundant, the Bible irrelevant, and salvation a state of mind. The story of the decline of vital religion, however, is much more complex.

As Darwin's popularizer, Spencer and his allies benefited enormously from The Myth of Progress that already had captured the Western imagination. There were many secular-minded thinkers and activists in the eugenics movement, but they received great moral support from religious leaders: ministers and others who discarded the historic teachings of the church and became beguiled by the Myth. At the same time, they eagerly enlisted the Bible to portray eugenics as a mandate from heaven. "The evidence yields a clear pattern about who elected to support eugenic-style reforms and who did not," writes Christine Rosen in *Preaching Eugenics*. "Religious leaders pursued eugenics precisely when they moved away from traditional religious tenets."[57]

This weakening of Christian belief occurred at the moment when Tolkien and Lewis were developing their own intellectual lives. They began their educations when The Myth of Progress was at a fever pitch, when it was widely believed that science— the science of eugenics—could perfect human nature and thus human societies.

It's important to remember that eugenicists thought of themselves as reformers, committed to improving the human condition. They endorsed the idea of state action to achieve their goals. "They were dedicated to facing head-on the challenges posed by modernity," writes Rosen. "Doing so meant embracing scientific solutions."[58] Animated by the Myth, they emphasized the collective destiny of the human race, at the expense of the individual. The conceit of the intellectual elites of the day was that science, and the technology it underwrites, could solve the most intractable of human problems.

Tolkien and Lewis encountered the horrific progeny of this thinking—in the trenches and barbed wire and mortars of the Great War—and it gave them great pause about human potentiality. On the one hand, the characters in their novels possess a great nobility: creatures endowed with a unique capacity for virtue, courage, and love. Indeed, a vital theme throughout is the sacred worth of the individual soul; in Middle-earth and in Narnia, every life is of immense consequence. On the other hand, their characters are deeply flawed individuals, capable of great evil, and in desperate need of divine grace to overcome their predicament. Both authors thus reflect the historic Christian tradition: human nature as a tragic mix of nobility and wretchedness.

As we'll see, this frankly religious doctrine—the biblical fall—was confirmed by their experience of war. It would supply the moral architecture for their stories, giving them an enduring sense of realism and relevance. "You come of the Lord Adam and the Lady Eve," Aslan tells Caspian in *The Chronicles of Narnia*. "And that is both honor enough to erect the head of the poorest beggar, and shame enough to bow the shoulders of the greatest emperor on earth."[59] Tolkien wrote that the idea of "the Fall of Man" lurked behind every story, and that "all stories are ultimately about the fall."[60]

THE MERCILESS MACHINERY OF WAR

The deep moral conundrum of *The Lord of the Rings*, of course, involves a weapon: a powerful Ring that could overcome the forces of evil arrayed against Middle-earth, yet which threatens to corrupt anyone who tries to use it, even those whose motives are pure. When Frodo is reunited with Bilbo at Rivendell, for example, he appears to encounter an individual momentarily distorted by his lust for the Ring. "To his distress and amazement he found that he was no longer looking at Bilbo; a shadow seemed to have fallen between them, and through it he found himself eyeing a little wrinkled creature with a hungry face and bony groping hands."[61]

In the opening pages of *The Magician's Nephew*, we meet Jadis, "the last Queen," a woman of immense wickedness. She holds the secret of "the Deplorable Word," a force that can destroy entire worlds, a power too terrible to contemplate. "What was it?" asks Digory. "That was the secret of secrets," says Jadis. "It had long been known to the great kings of our race that there was a word which, if spoken with the proper ceremonies, would destroy all living things except the one who spoke it. . . . I learned it in a secret place and paid a terrible price to learn it."[62]

Perhaps this was the most terrifying result of The Myth of Progress: it inspired great advances in military technology, but failed to advance any new theories of warfare to address the consequences of this technology on the battlefield. The years leading up to the First World War initiated a new era of military planning, for example, in which the modern European rail network enabled the swift mobilization of troops and armaments. This by itself amounted to a revolution in how the next conflict would be fought.

Yet when war arrived in August 1914, hardly anyone grasped what the human costs would be. Observes historian Niall Ferguson: "Suddenly, the vast resources of the European industrial economies were diverted from production to destruction."[63]

Ironically, among the fruits of industrialization were rising health and living standards, which allowed for rapid population growth—and larger and more destructive armies. There were millions more young men available for military service than ever before. At the outbreak of the war, Germany would quickly mobilize 715,000 men, Austria 600,000, France 400,000, and Russia more than a million. Even Great Britain, with its all-volunteer army, would call up 165,000 troops.

Now, thanks to science and technology, soldiers could be shuttled into war zones—ten times faster by rail than by horse and foot—on a timetable as precise as a Swiss watch. In England, in the space of five days, eighteen hundred special trains ran south to Southampton, one arriving every three minutes for sixteen hours a day. Fourteen French railways carried fifty-six trains a day. Trains could deliver men to and from the front lines as if they were shift-workers in a factory.[64] By an "inflexible calculation," writes John Keegan, military planners would dictate how many troops could be carried at what speed to any designated border zone. "Trains were to fill the memories of all who went to war in 1914."[65]

On June 28, 1914, an assassin's bullet in Sarajevo set a vast political-military machine into motion. By midnight on August 4, five empires were at war: the German Empire against Britain, France, and Russia; the Austro-Hungarian Empire against Serbia; the Russian Empire against Germany and Austria-Hungary; and the British and French Empires against Germany. Each side was confident, supremely confident, of swift victory. Just as French troops expected to reach Berlin before the fall, so the Germans believed they would parade down the Champs-Elysee in Paris in six weeks. Observes historian Sir Martin Gilbert: "It was a careful, precise, and comforting calculation."[66]

The Myth of Progress that made such calculations conceivable also created the instruments of war that would render them horribly obsolete. Neither the generals nor the politicians were thinking in moral terms about the consequences of mechanized warfare.

Battleships, submarines, the motorized transport of troops, the heavy siege howitzers, the machine guns, tanks, barbed wire, poison gas, flamethrowers, the thousands of miles of trenches— all of this awaited the soldiers of the Great War. The mass production of artillery became a kind of holy grail throughout the conflict. Advances in the destructive power of explosives and in the size, mobility, and accuracy of artillery meant that shocking numbers of men could be killed from long distances, without ever seeing what hit them. Hence the construction of trenches along the Western Front and the beginning of a war of attrition. Almost immediately the war was described "like a colossal machine, chewing up men and munitions like so much raw material."[67]

"There was every expectation that the conflict would be brief, that the latest military technology would limit the scale of damage on all sides," writes W. M. Spellman. "Indeed many viewed the prospect of a general war as cathartic and cleansing. War would renew each nation's sense of purpose while liberating factory workers, farmers, office clerks, and students from their dull workaday activities, the complacency of bourgeois existence."[68]

Instead, the war would last longer, and be fought with greater savagery, than anyone dared to imagine. The mutilated bodies of numberless millions of factory workers, farmers, clerks, and students would be consigned to graves scattered throughout Europe. The smallest villages, with their proud and austere cemeteries, still bear witness to their own part in the conflict.

In the main *piazza* in Bitritto, where my grandfather Michele was born, there is a memorial to the *caduti*, the fallen in battle, Even my grandfather Giuseppe's home of Ventotene—a tiny and obscure island in the Tyrrhenian Sea—has a monument in its *piazza* to those who perished *"nella grande guerra."*

WHEN THE LIGHTS GO OUT

The early apostles of The Myth of Progress believed they had overcome the problems of industrial society. More than that, they imagined that they had solved the riddle of human existence.

"Progress, visible in every facet of life and ruling as the governing force behind existence, brought order to a world of change and moral purpose to a universe otherwise disturbingly random and meaningless," writes historian Richard Gamble. "This faith in progress anchored the soul."[69] A generation later, the leaders of England and the rest of Europe assumed that their science, education, philanthropy, gentility, and religion represented the future of Western civilization. Even war would serve to advance the destiny of humanity. "Their confident belief in progress and the idea that enlightened self-interest would bring harmony to the whole world was, in retrospect, an illusion," concludes Roger Osborne. "By the end of the nineteenth century Britain and Europe were heading not to a better society, but towards the catastrophe of mechanized warfare."[70]

Two of the twentieth century's most influential Christian writers were caught up in this illusion, their lives transformed in its wake. Much of their literary output would be a response to the assumptions that not only made the Great War possible, but added mightily to its destructive and vindictive power. The long shadows cast by this conflict do not fail to touch the borders of the Shire and of Narnia.

Such is the force of The Myth of Progress: even as its funeral oration was being written in the cabinet rooms of every major European capital, its power and promise would continue to deceive many. Yet not all. The day that Britain declared war on Germany, British Foreign Secretary Sir Edward Grey was standing with a friend in Whitehall, looking out his window across St. James Park. It was dusk. As he watched the gas lamps below being lit, he grew somber.

"The lamps are going out all over Europe," he said. "We shall not see them lit again in our lifetime."[71]

CHAPTER 2

THE LAST BATTLE

B ritish historian C. V. Wedgwood, writing twenty years after the conclusion of the First World War, produced a sweeping survey of a conflict that created a human catastrophe for Europe. She drew her wounding observations to a close with an economy and power of language that has few rivals: "Morally subversive, economically destructive, socially degrading, confused in its causes, devious in its course, futile in its result, it is the outstanding example in European history of meaningless conflict."[1]

Wedgwood's account, however, was not about the deadly conflagration that had engulfed the Continent just a generation earlier. The war she had in mind was fought in the early seventeenth century. It has been called Europe's last religious war: the Thirty Years War.

The Protestant Reformation not only shattered the religious unity of Europe: it set in motion a long period of sectarian violence that divided the Continent into rival political-religious empires.

What began in 1618 as a conflict between Catholic and Protestant forces in the German province of Bohemia spiraled into a vast, Machiavellian struggle for dynastic power and real estate.

In a certain sense, the conflict anticipated the Great War. Although it could have remained a regional dispute, it sucked into its vortex most of the nations of Europe. Like the First World War, the Thirty Years War was breathtaking in its scope and destructive power. Like its twentieth-century counterpart, it resulted in startling numbers of casualties, caused massive physical devastation, disrupted local economies, and threatened the social fabric of European civilization. In modern-day Germany, where much of the fight occurred, the mortality rate—from combat, famine, and disease—was about 20 percent of the entire population.

The wretched memories of the conflict, real or imagined, never left the European mind. "The Thirty Years War became the benchmark to measure all later wars," writes Peter Wilson in *The Thirty Years War: Europe's Tragedy.* "Soldiers fighting in the trenches along the eastern front of the First World War believed they were experiencing horrors not seen in three centuries."[2]

The Treaty of Westphalia (1648) not only ended the conflict, but sought to remove religion as a source of political strife. Westphalia set a new political foundation for the West, based on the sovereignty of the state, the right of non-interference in internal (religious) affairs, and the idea of international law to settle disputes. Pope Innocent X rejected Westphalia for limiting the authority of the Church, calling the treaty "null, void, invalid, iniquitous, unjust, damnable, reprobate, inane, empty of meaning and effect for all time."[3]

The pope lost the argument, though, and the Treaty of Westphalia essentially created "a new charter for European relations" that survived up until the First World War.[4] Under Westphalia, the secular interests of the state would set the course of international affairs. The nations of Europe had finally put an end to wars motivated by religious belief.

DUTY, PATRIOTISM, AND MUSCULAR RELIGION

Or had they? In fact, Westphalia failed to permanently tame the passions of sectarian religion. Almost from the outbreak of hostilities, the First World War became a conflict infused with religious themes. What might have remained a regional skirmish over ethnic self-determination became something like an apocalyptic contest between the forces of Good and Evil.

"Whatever the local agendas, Christians in all combatant nations—including the United States—entered wholeheartedly in the spirit of cosmic war," writes Philip Jenkins in *The Great and Holy War*. "None found any difficulty in using fundamental tenets of the faith as warrants to justify war and mass destruction."[5] The zeal of Arthur Winnington-Ingram, the influential Bishop of London, was not unusual among the clergy of Great Britain: "I think the Church can best help the nation first of all by making it realize that it is engaged in a Holy War, and not be afraid of saying so," he wrote. "Christ died on Good Friday for Freedom, Honor and Chivalry, and our boys are dying for the same things . . . MOBILIZE THE NATION FOR A HOLY WAR!"[6]

J. R. R. Tolkien and C. S. Lewis became part of this mobilization. They enlisted as officers in the British army, trained for combat, and dispatched to France in 1916–17. As young boys, they had been sent away to English preparatory schools: Tolkien at King Edward's School in Birmingham, while Lewis went to Cherbourg School in Great Malvern. These institutions were incubators of Victorian virtues: duty, honor, patriotism, and religion. Christianity and love of England went hand in hand, but the emphasis was on *duty*—duty to king and country—not on belief.[7]

England's public school system reinforced these values in various ways, not least of which occurred on the soccer field. Sportsmanship was a means of maintaining a martial spirit, tethered to patriotic duty. "The sports field was an arena for feigned combat," writes biographer John Garth. "In the books most boys read, war was sport continued by other means."[8] Sportsmanship was an expression of "muscular Christianity," an assertive form of faith that reinforced the manlier civic virtues. "The sporting spirit, at its best," according to one chaplain, "is the highest form of the Christian spirit attainable by men at our present stage of development."[9]

Lacking interest or ability in athletics, Lewis rejected the martial culture of Malvern College, where he had begun studies in 1914. "These brutes of illiterate, ill-managed English prefects," he wrote his father, "are always watching for an opportunity to drop upon you."[10] Lewis found sanctuary in the school library and threw himself into literature and the arts. "We shall not understand Jack," writes biographer George Sayer, "unless we can appreciate his gift for being utterly absorbed in the imaginative world of a great writer, artist, or musician."[11] It was during this time that Lewis developed this gift, and it soon drew him into all kinds of works, from Dante's *Inferno* to Norse mythologies to Malory's *Morte d'Arthur*. After he began reading Homer's *Iliad* in the original Greek, he wrote his friend Arthur Greeves:

"Although you don't know Greek and don't care for poetry, I cannot resist the temptation of telling you how stirring it is."[12]

Tolkien, on the other hand, served as captain of the rugby team at King Edward's, and he and many of its members became cadets in the recently established Officer Training Corps. It was at King Edward's, where Latin and Greek formed the backbone of the curriculum, that Tolkien developed his love for languages. "It was just as the 1914 War burst upon me that I made the discovery that 'legends' depend on the language to which they belong," he wrote later. "But a living language depends equally on the 'legends' which it conveys by tradition."[13] Tolkien became absorbed by Joseph Wright's *Primer of the Gothic Language* (and later was tutored by Wright). He read in the original Old English the warrior poem *Beowulf*, a medieval tale of "a man at war with the hostile world," a theme that would define his literary career.[14]

Although both men read and enjoyed stories about war, about armies clashing in a great moral contest, they did not think of themselves as "holy crusaders" when the First World War got underway. Tolkien did not get swept up in the war fever of 1914. When tens of thousands of young men volunteered for service in the British Expeditionary Force, he continued his studies. In August 1916, shortly after being deployed to France, Tolkien experienced the "universal weariness" of war and the "bitter disillusionment" of discovering that his military training had not prepared him for the conditions of actual combat.[15]

Some of Lewis's journal entries during this time record his anxiety about being wounded in the war.[16] Almost until the day of his enlistment, in fact, he hoped he could avoid military service.[17] He remarked wryly to his father that one of the most serious consequences of the war was the survival of those least fit for survival. "All those who have the courage to do so and are physically sound, are going off to be shot: those who survive are moral and physical weeds—a fact which does not promise favorably for the next generation."[18]

Based on their letters and journals, it is certain that neither man saw himself as a potential martyr in a holy war, or even viewed the conflict as an opportunity for martial glory. What Tolkien and Lewis probably absorbed from their education was an understanding of England's role in defending the ideals of Western civilization. Britain's common-law tradition, judicial system, parliamentary government, and Bill of Rights were among the great contributions to human progress. Its alliances in Europe served not only British national interests, but helped to safeguard the peace and security of the Continent. "It spread and enforced the rule of law over vast areas," writes Niall Ferguson. "Though it fought many small wars, the Empire maintained a global peace unmatched before or since."[19] As one war veteran described it: "I suppose at no time did one live so much with a consciousness of the past."[20]

British history made patriotic duty plausible to most Englishmen. "I could not pray for a finer death," wrote J. Engall, serving on the Western Front with the 16th London Regiment, "and you my dear Mother and Father, will know that I died doing my duty to my God, my Country, and my King."[21] Whatever their other motivations, British soldiers in the First World War believed they were defending the values and institutions essential to human flourishing. "In Britain and France duty was associated with honor and loyalty and a fight for civilized and civilizing values, such as justice and dignity and freedom from tyranny," explains historian

Modris Eksteins. "Hence duty was not an abstract notion at the beginning of the war. It was a practical imperative."[22]

Germany's unprovoked aggression in Belgium created the imperative. Britain had signed a treaty with Belgium in 1839, guaranteeing its neutrality in the event of a European conflict. After Germany declared war on France, London issued Berlin an ultimatum not to invade Belgium. But the Kaiser ignored the warning and masses of German troops poured across the border.

Within hours Great Britain was at war with Germany. Prime Minister Herbert Henry Asquith, addressing the House of Commons on August 6, 1914, emphasized the nation's political and moral commitments: "I do not believe any nation ever entered into a greater controversy . . . with a clearer conscience and a stronger conviction that it is fighting, not for aggression, not for the maintenance of its own selfish interest, but that it is fighting in defense of principles, the maintenance of which is vital to the civilization of the world."[23] If the First World War became something like a religious war, it did not begin this way.

A MODERN CRUSADE

The ethos of patriotism and muscular faith could serve a noble purpose. It conditioned a generation of young men for the unprecedented sacrifices of the First World War. From the opening days of the conflict, however, British clergymen seized upon this ethos and transformed it into something more: the doctrine of the holy war.

Under this vision, the aims of the state became almost identical to those of the church. Practically speaking, this meant that political and military objectives were given a religious rationale, backed up by the Bible. Britain was by no means unique in this regard: every combatant nation adopted more or less the same posture. Religious leaders across national and religious lines became fervent defenders of the war effort. "Clergymen dressed Jesus in khaki and had him firing machine guns," writes one historian. "The war became one not of justice but of righteousness."[24] In sermons, books, articles, and pamphlets, they portrayed the conflict as a holy crusade: a spiritual battle against a demonic foe with whom no compromise was possible.

How do we explain it? The reasons were complex; the influence of Christianity in society, of course, looked different in Britain, France, Russia, Germany, Austria-Hungary, and elsewhere in Europe. Nevertheless, the European states all had long traditions of "national" or "established" churches, meaning state support for a favored Christian denomination. The alliance of church and state allowed the secular goals of government to get mixed up with spiritual goals of Christianity.

Add to this the rise of the most potent political ideology of the hour: nationalism. The nation-state was replacing religion as a powerful source of meaning and identity in people's lives. "Nationalism effortlessly incorporated some of the major themes of the Judeo-Christian tradition," writes Michael Burleigh in *Earthly Powers: Religion and Politics in Europe from the French Revolution to the Great War*. This included "the belief that a people had been chosen to fulfill a providential purpose."[25]

For devoted nationalists, their patriotic faith was equivalent to membership in an alternative church. For religious believers, nationalism offered a grandiose political outlet for their faith commitments. The result was the birth of Christian nationalism, the near sanctification of the modern state.

In his classic critique of British foreign policy, *Imperialism* (1902), J. A. Hobson accused the Church of England of invariably giving its blessing to the nation's military adventures. "In England the State Church has never permitted the spirit of the Prince of Peace to interfere when statesmen and soldiers appealed to the passions of race-lust, conquest, and revenge."[26] Although not accurate—church leaders could take the government to task for its moral lapses—the charge was by no means groundless. As the established church, the Church of England was integral to the British state and most often sided with King and Parliament on issues concerning the national interest.

The situation was much the same in Germany, where Protestant clerics received government support and, in turn, tended to support the state in its domestic and foreign policy. Thus, in September 1914, a group of ninety-three leading German intellectuals, including many theologians, issued a declaration endorsing without qualification the Kaiser's war policy as essential to the defense of Christian civilization.[27] Catholic clergy in France followed a similar pattern. Even ministers in the United States, with no established church, caught war fever. Such was the crusading mood on both sides of the Atlantic that even religious groups active in the peace movement at the turn of the century gave themselves fully to the cause.

The Christian nationalism that characterized the religious communities of Europe, however, only partly explains this enthusiasm. To it must be added The Myth of Progress that, as we've seen, functioned for many like a substitute faith. Many religious believers—especially those drifting away from historic Christianity—adopted its secular aims and assumptions. "One thing is clear: the future of the world is democratic, and nothing can stop it," proclaimed a London minister. "Progress is by Divine authority, by Divine necessity; God is the great innovator."[28]

ENGLAND AS THE SALT OF THE EARTH

As Christian clergy transformed themselves into holy warriors, one theme appeared in common among the combatants: the belief that their nations were specially chosen by Providence to accomplish his progressive purposes on the world stage. Fidelity to God demanded fidelity to one's country as God's instrument, especially in wartime. Cross and Crown must be kept together.

In England, this idea could be traced as far back as the English Reformation, launched in the 1530s under Henry VIII. Once Protestantism, embodied in the Anglican Church, became the nation's official religion, church and state joined in common cause against Catholicism. As such, they represented a new and vital front in the advance of God's kingdom. "This schema," writes historian John Spurr, "gave a leading role to the godly prince, the new Constantine, whose task it was to further the Reformation, take on Antichrist and hasten the final apocalypse."[29]

By the time of the Glorious Revolution (1689), Great Britain's self-identity as an exceptional nation—as a nation chosen by God for holy purposes—was secure. The First World War revealed that the concept was alive and well, at least among many of the clergy. "Who are we?" asked John Hancock in *God's Dealings with the British Empire* (1916). In answering, Handcock piled one biblical image on top of another. "We are God's chosen people, His inheritance, the salt of the earth, His loved ones, His glory, the people He delights in, His sons and His daughters. What more can we wish for?"[30]

Likewise, T. W. Crafer, vicar of All Saints Church, Cambridge, saw England, like Israel, as the apple of God's eye. "We believe that we are a nation wondrously favored by God, and we like to think of ourselves as a chosen people, whose name stands in the world for righteousness and peace." An empire as powerful as Great Britain, he reasoned, fighting to defend the weak against the strong, "must be a precious instrument for good in the hands of God."[31] The wartime advocacy of Bishop Winnington-Ingram, as described by his biographer, probably applied to the majority of English clergymen: "There was for him a sacredness about England which was beyond argument. . . . His instinctive judgment was that the national cause must be right."[32]

Britons of all classes could point to their empire's many accomplishments: its lead role in abolishing the international slave trade, its expanding panoply of human liberties, its united commonwealth, its civilizing influence wherever the Union Jack found safe harbor. Under this view, England was "the polished arrow" in the quiver of the Almighty, a nation with a special task in the world.[33]

It was the English clergy, though, that transformed the political-military task of punishing German aggression into a righteous crusade: a struggle between Christianity and paganism. Ministers of the Church of England, as servants of God and of the state, became some of the most effective recruiting agents during the war.[34]

AMERICA AS A CITY ON A HILL

The concept of America as an exceptional nation is as old as the republic, and older still. Ever since John Winthrop and his band of Puritans landed at Massachusetts Bay in 1630, Americans have thought of themselves as pilgrims on a divine "errand in the wilderness," destined to establish a holy commonwealth and "a city on a hill."

This theme reappears constantly, framing the nation's political crises beginning with the American Revolution. Evangelical ministers blessed the cause of independence from their pulpits throughout the war.

Preaching before the Connecticut General Assembly, Ezra Stiles used Deuteronomy 26:19 to address "the political welfare of God's American Israel."[35] The most rationalistic of the American Founders—including Benjamin Franklin, Thomas Jefferson, and John Adams—argued in much the same terms. "Their God was intimately involved in the events of American history," writes Conrad Cherry in *God's New Israel.* "Divine Providence was the force that moved the United States to liberty; eventually providence would, through the example of the United States, direct the world to the same end."[36]

Thus, on April 2, 1917, when Woodrow Wilson delivered his brief to Congress for American intervention in the First World War, he echoed the themes of American Exceptionalism that had inspired virtually every president before him. He said it was America's privilege to "spend her blood and her might" for the principles of liberty and justice upon which the nation was founded. Leading a concert of peace-loving nations, the United States "shall bring peace and safety to all nations and make the world itself at last free." Paraphrasing Martin Luther's rebuttal to ecclesiastical tyranny at the Diet of Worms, he concluded: "God helping her, she can do no other."[37]

Wilson came to office promising to keep America out of a

European war. His conversion set off the equivalent of a tent revival meeting among the nation's clergy. Monsignor C. F. Thomas, speaking at St. Patrick's Church in Washington DC, saw the Divine hand at work in America's historic commitment to democratic ideals. "The Providence of God destines this nation to last—indefinitely, we confidently trust," he said. "The whole world looks to us to carry to the future what will save the future from disorder, confusion, anarchy, perhaps dissolution. But our trust cannot be fulfilled without the loyalty, love, personal and patriotic efforts of each and every individual."[38]

Samuel Zane Batten, a Baptist preacher and secretary of the Northern Baptist Convention's War Commission, attached deep spiritual significance to America's engagement: "This war for the destruction of injustice of inhumanity is a holy crusade and a continuation of Christ's sacrificial service for the redemption of the world."[39] Likewise, Randolph McKim, a Presbyterian minister in Washington DC, put the war in essentially apocalyptic terms: "This conflict is indeed a crusade. The greatest in history—the holiest. It is in the profoundest and truest sense a Holy War. . . . Yes, it is Christ, the King of Righteousness, who calls us to grapple in deadly strife with this unholy and blasphemous power."[40]

GERMANY: GOD IS WITH US

Germany under the Kaiser was even more brazen about associating its political claims with the Divine Will. In Berlin, Emperor Wilhelm II, who also served as supreme bishop of the Prussian Church, delivered this message to his troops at the outbreak of war: "Remember that the German people are the chosen of

God. On me, on me as German Emperor, the Spirit of God has descended. I am His weapon. His sword and His visor. . . . Death to cowards and unbelievers!"[41]

The problem in Germany went much deeper than an eccentric Kaiser. Taking Christian nationalism to its logical conclusion, many pastors equated Christianity with the German *Volk*. "The German national soul is saturated with the spirit of God," proclaimed Gottfried Naumann. "We fight for this soul on behalf of the world, because we know that it is a work of God and contains God's blessings for the entire world."[42] Theologian Ernst Troeltsch made no distinction between the will of a "divine world ruler" and German culture. "Our faith is not just that we can and must defend our state and homeland but that our national essence contains an inexhaustible richness and value that are inexpressibly important for mankind, a value that the Lord and God of history has entrusted to our protection and development."[43]

In *Earthly Powers*, historian Michael Burleigh suggests that liberal Protestant theologians, by emphasizing the "immanence" or immediate presence of God, were prone to confuse the *Volksgeist* with the Holy Spirit. Their theology "meant that He was manifest in the intense emotions of August 1914, directing the movements of German armies at war."[44]

The outpouring of support among the German people for war—and the apparent return of worshippers to formerly empty churches—seemed to signal a New Pentecost. Ministers spoke of an *Offenbarung*, or "revelation," as well as *Verklärung*, or "transfiguration," to describe the war's effects on the national climate. The slogan *Gott mit uns* (God with us) became a favorite expression of the German people.[45] "Germany's Protestant preachers and theologians frankly exulted in the outbreak of war," writes Philip Jenkins. "Christian leaders treated the war as a spiritual event, in which their nation was playing a messianic role in Europe and the world."[46]

THE BEAST OF BERLIN

If the nations of Europe and the United States were indeed engaged in a holy war, then their enemies were God's enemies as well; they were the minions of the Evil One. And if Scripture was any guide, there could be no surrender, no compromise with the forces of evil—only a total war to defeat them.

As leader of the Central Powers, the German "Hun" became the principal object of vilification among the Allied nations. In a popular war tract, American writer Elbert Hubbard pressed home this question: "Who lifted the lid off of hell?"[47] Fundamentalist preacher Billy Sunday, as incendiary as a Molotov cocktail, spoke for clerics on both sides of the Atlantic: "If you turn Hell upside down, you'll find 'Made in Germany' stamped on the bottom."

Before examining the contribution of the churches to the demonization campaign, we should remember that Germany authorized numerous acts of aggression and vindictive violence that outraged the democratic Allies. After German troops invaded Belgium, reports of atrocities against civilians filtered out of the country: massacres, the use of women and children as human shields, rape, the mistreatment and execution of prisoners, and other war crimes. C. S. Lewis wrote his father in October 1914, mentioning a friend who was "employed at his camp the other day in unloading a train of seriously wounded soldiers from the front: from whom he learned that the newspaper stories of

German atrocities (mutilation of nurses, killing wounded, etc.) were not in the least exaggerated."[48]

Exaggeration or not, to the English clergy this was "savagery reduced to a science." Britain established the Bryce Commission to investigate the allegations. Though its assessment of German guilt was severely criticized after the war, the commission was essentially correct in its major conclusions. "These were not just the actions of soldiers out of control of their officers," writes historian Dan Todman in *The Great War: Myth and Memory.* "German atrocities were a matter of policy, not just panic."[49]

The Germans blackened their reputation further when they sliced their way into northern France. German troops savaged the historic library of Louvain and destroyed the Gothic cathedral of Rheims, known as "the Parthenon of France." In February 1915, German U-boats attacked commercial vessels, essentially declaring that Germany would make no distinction between military and civilian targets.

Germany was also the first nation to use chemical weapons on the battlefield. On April 22, at Ypres, the Germans released 168 tons of chlorine gas along a four-mile front. French troops watched "awestruck and dumbfounded" as a grey-green mist washed over them, filling the eyes, nose, and throat with a noxious odor.[50] By preventing the lungs from absorbing oxygen, chlorine causes its victims to slowly drown in their own fluids. Thrown into a panic—none of the French soldiers knew what the gas was—men fled for their lives. The advancing Germans were stunned by the scene: five thousand enemy soldiers on their backs, gasping for air, suffocating in agony and terror.[51]

To the Allies, all of this symbolized a German assault on the values of Western civilization. By May 1915, when the Bryce

Commission report was translated into thirty languages, an image of German militarism, barbarism, and *realpolitik* run amok was set in stone.

Even so, G. A. Studdert Kennedy, one of Britain's best-known chaplains, encouraged soldiers on the front by applying the Bible in ways that offend modern sensibilities: "A traitor friend betrayed the Christ . . . a traitor nation has crucified the world!" As Studdert Kennedy saw it, the Germans had debased Christian morality and replaced it with the values of brute force and paganism: "The god the German leaders worship is an idol of the earth—a crude and cruel monster who lives on human blood."[52]

James Plowden-Wardlaw, Vicar of St. Clement's in Cambridge, accused the Kaiser and his army of worshipping Satan in the form of a Prussian tribal god. "How angels must weep," he said, "to see the tragedy of the fall, the moral fall, of Germany."[53] Many ministers insisted that the war bring about "a complete end" to the German system: "The world can never be safe until this new cancer is cut clean out of the body of humanity."[54] As the war dragged on, references in sermons and religious literature to the biblical end times grew more frequent. H. C. Beeching, Dean of Norwich, offered a typical indictment against Germany and its allies: "We are fighting for others as well as for ourselves . . . for Christ against anti-Christ," he wrote. "And so the battle is not ours, it is indeed Armageddon. Ranged against us are the Dragon and the False Prophet."[55]

Once the United States entered the war against Germany, American clergymen became as zealous as their British counterparts. For many, the German chancellor represented a unique embodiment of moral evil.

George Holley Gilbert, a Congregational minister, saw "a

thoroughly militarized Christianity, like that of the Kaiser, as the lowest and most harmful religion ever developed on earth."[56] Methodist bishop Richard Cooke explained that "the real reason for the war" was "to vindicate God Almighty against the brutal philosophy of damned men."[57] Even academics such as James Day, chancellor at Syracuse University, could not resist using religious language to condemn German militarism. "It would be a blessing," he said, "if we could turn the beast of Berlin over to God and say, 'Lord, inflict violent wrath upon this creature.'"[58]

POLITICAL AND SPIRITUAL REDEMPTION

A holy war against an unholy power: the result, according to the Allied clergy, would be nothing less than the political and spiritual rebirth of Western culture. The autocracies and petty kingdoms of Europe would give way to the self-governing ideals of liberal democracy. Materialism would yield to the spiritual values of Christianity.

Some churchmen viewed the war as God's verdict on the growing secularism and materialism of the West. "Perhaps God has allowed us to pull down the temple of modern civilization over our heads," explained Percy Dearmer, "in order that the survivors may be cured of the modern habit of regarding man as a calculating machine."[59] For others, the war would propel the steady evolution of democratic societies.

Returning from a diplomatic mission to Russia in 1917, former U.S. Secretary of State Elihu Root went on a nationwide lecture tour, telling audiences that America was destined to lead "the upward progress of humanity along the pathway of civilization to a true Christian life."[60] David Cairns, professor of apologetics at Aberdeen, suggested that a new era of international peace was dawning. "We cannot see the world-situation tonight, or indeed at any time, unless we dream a little about the future," he said. "I am willing to dream that we are going to have not only a concert of Europe, but a concert of the world for a great common end."[61]

Advocates of the social gospel were especially hopeful: they imagined the war as a cleansing experience, a means to purge entire societies of their sub-Christian loyalties. An Allied victory would ensure a progressive future for the United States and Europe. Lyman Abbott, one of the best-known liberal theologians of his day, envisioned "progressive redemption" as a result of the war. Americans were working hard "to banish those crimes against humanity from our civilization," he said, and to bring about "the triumph for Christianity such as the world has never before known."[62]

In *The War for Righteousness: Progressive Christianity, the Great War, and the Rise of the Messianic Nation*, historian Richard Gamble argues that progressive clergy were particularly prone to convert the conflict into a culturally and spiritually transformative event. "They seized upon the war as an opportunity to reconstruct the churches, America, and the world according to the imperatives of the social gospel," he writes. "Their peacetime crusade became a wartime crusade."[63]

The expectation of widespread cultural renewal was broadcast from America's "bully pulpit" on January 8, 1918, when Woodrow Wilson announced his Fourteen Points for the establishment of global peace and security after the war. At the moral center of Wilson's vision was a global political community based on trust and mutual regard: the diplomatic application of the Golden Rule.

Almost without exception, church leaders became tireless evangelists for Wilson's gospel of peaceful internationalism. "The world that existed before the War has disappeared forever," declared John Mott. "For the world it is a new birth, a great day of God such as comes only once in 100 or 1,000 years."[64] Joseph Fort Newton, a famous minister at London's City Temple, likewise discerned "a new chapter in the social, political, intellectual and spiritual life of mankind."

In *The Sword of the Spirit: Britain and America in the Great War* (1918), Newton likened the war to the Christian Crusades of medieval Europe. Just as the earlier crusaders had unified Europe, he predicted, "so this, the greatest humanitarian crusade in history, will unify the world." The advance of humankind would proceed "slowly, surely, inevitably" as national hatreds and sectarian pettiness "yield to the pressure of world-obligation and community of interest." In the end, Newton assured his readers, "men will think in terms of one humanity and one Christianity."[65]

The attainment of such a world, of course, depended on the utter defeat and humiliation of the enemy. There could be no room for compromise or limited objectives. The Christmas truce along the Western Front in December 1914 would never be duplicated. All this helps explain the opposition of many church leaders to peace proposals that would have left Germany undefeated and unpunished. Concludes Gamble: "It was a war for absolutes that combined the armies of heaven and earth into the ultimate battle."[66]

Here, then, is one of the most striking effects of the Myth

of Progress. Even war itself—a process inherently destructive to human life and human societies—was believed to have regenerative properties. The assumption of religious leaders in England and the United States was that war would advance the ideals of Christianity and democracy. More than that, it would give birth to an epoch of peace and righteousness: the "last battle" before the dawn of a new world. Whatever the religious beliefs of the combatants, the secular idealism of the Myth was driving attitudes and expectations about the conflict's outcome.

The problem, of course, was that none of these holy predictions would come to pass. The gulf between the prophecies of the clergymen and the realities of the conflict would overshadow many souls in the postwar generation. Paul Bull, a minister and former chaplain, spoke for many of them: "The Age of Progress ends in a barbarism such as shocks a savage. The Age of Reason ends in a delirium of madness."[67]

FAITH IN THE TRENCHES

Two young soldiers, J. R. R. Tolkien and C. S. Lewis, managed to survive this delirium with their souls intact. It is not easy to say how the temper of the times shaped their attitudes as they went off to war; no person fully escapes the assumptions of his age. Nevertheless, neither man ever expressed the crusader mind-set, much less the apocalyptic views of the clergy. Their goals were much more practical and earthly: to fight honorably, survive the trenches intact, and pick up their academic careers where the war had interrupted them. "Before I went to the last war I certainly expected that my life in the trenches would, in some mysterious sense, be all war," wrote Lewis years later. "In fact, I found that the nearer you got to the front line the less everyone spoke and thought of the allied cause and the progress of the campaign."[68]

In this, Tolkien and Lewis probably shared the sentiments of the majority of their fellow soldiers.[69] Many were outraged by German atrocities and loathed the idea of German hegemony in Europe. Yet there is little evidence that the ordinary soldier was animated by intense religious idealism. A story circulated in France, for example, about a clergyman in a carriage of men on their way to the front line. He cheerfully asks them, "So, you are going to fight God's war?" After getting no reply, he repeats the question. "Don't you believe in God's war?" A soldier looks at him wearily and replies: "Sir, hadn't you better keep your poor Friend out of this bloody mess?"[70]

Unfortunately for the Church of England, many chaplains were out of sight and apparently out of touch during the war. Ordered to remain safely behind the lines, at hospitals or field ambulances, they often seemed incapable of relating to the men fighting for survival.

"The key to the whole thing," wrote Theodore Hardy, a chaplain who later won the Victoria Cross, was for ministers to serve in the combat zone: "If you stay back, you are wasting your time. Men will forgive anything but lack of courage." Most Protestant ministers, however, followed orders and avoided the front. "There is only one Front here and few Chaplains ever get there, and then not during engagements," complained David Railton. "It is a mistake on the part of the authorities which will cost the Church dearly."[71]

Perhaps it did. Many Anglican chaplains worked courageously to serve the men under their care. Of the two thousand Anglican clergy attached to the British army at the time of the Armistice, eighty-eight died in battle, while four were awarded the Victoria Cross.[72] Nevertheless, war poet Robert Graves—his cynicism aside—seemed to capture a common perception of clerical cowardice and hypocrisy: "If they had shown one-tenth the courage, endurance, and other human qualities that the regimental doctors showed, we agreed, the British Expeditionary Force might well have started a religious revival."[73] Despite great hopes to the contrary, no widespread revival occurred.[74]

For most men, it seems, God remained in the backdrop of the conflict, but not wholly absent. The oft-quoted critique by Graves—"hardly one soldier in a hundred was inspired by religious feeling of even the crudest kind"—seems a self-serving projection of his own militant atheism.[75] As historian Richard Schweitzer argues in *The Cross and the Trenches*, a strong percentage of soldiers referred to religious belief in their letters and diaries, suggesting genuine piety.[76] Perhaps the observation of a Scottish officer was closer to the mark: "The religion of ninety percent of the men at the front is not distinctively Christian," he wrote, "but a religion of patriotism and of valor, tinged with chivalry, and the best merely colored with sentiment and emotion borrowed from Christianity."[77]

CHASTENED BY WAR

On the eve of the Battle of the Somme, Douglas Haig, commander of the British Expeditionary Force, wrote to his wife: "I feel that every step in my plan has been taken with the Divine help."[78] Haig was convinced that his soldiers shared his simple faith and were similarly inspired to bear the sufferings required to prevail.[79] Harold Macmillan, a future prime minister who fought at Ypres in May 1916, was not prone to expressions of sectarian zeal. Nevertheless, he wrote to his mother: "Many of us could never stand the strain and endure the horrors which we see every day, if we did not feel that this was more than a war—a Crusade. I never see a man killed but think of him as a martyr."[80]

Did the experience of war transform Tolkien and Lewis into faith-based crusaders? Tolkien entered the war a devout Catholic, Lewis a lapsed Anglican and an atheist (his turn toward Christianity did not occur until much later). They shared a basic patriotism and sense of duty to King and Country, yet they were reluctant recruits into the war effort. As authors they sought to recover the romantic and mythic traditions based on the struggle between good and evil. But they declined to sanctify war as a divine undertaking. Rather, the characters in their works often display a great ambivalence toward conflict.

In *The Fellowship of the Ring*, Elrond grows somber as he reflects on the history of the wars that have ravaged his world. He has lived long enough to know that, despite hopes to the contrary, the forces of evil would not be eradicated by the next battle: "I have seen three ages in the West of the world, and many defeats, and many fruitless victories."[81] Tolkien denied that his *Lord of the Rings* was "just a plain fight between Good and Evil," or that his protagonists represent untainted goodness. "But in any case this is a tale about war," he wrote, "and if war is allowed (at least as a topic and a setting) it is not much good complaining that all the people on one side are against those on the other."[82]

Lewis occasionally poked fun at his characters, such as Reepicheep in the Narnia series, for their bravado: "For his mind was full of forlorn hopes, death-or-glory charges, and last stands."[83] In his science fiction trilogy, he created a mad Anglican parson, Mr. Straik, who naively endorses an earthly (and diabolical) attempt to realize the kingdom of God. "It is the beginning of Man Immortal and Man Ubiquitous," intones Straik. "Man on the throne of the universe. It is what all the prophecies really meant."[84] Straik might well have been modeled on any number of WWI ministers enchanted by the prospects of spiritual revival.

Indeed, what sets their works apart is how they avoid the triumphalism of the holy warrior. Tolkien deliberately submerged the Christian elements of his story, making even the idea of God only a suggestive aspect of the narrative. "Even when I was far away," says Gandalf, "there has never been a day when the Shire has not been guarded by watchful eyes."[85] Lewis was much more explicit about the biblical themes that frame his work. But even his protagonists—obedient to a Calling larger than themselves—are nonetheless flawed, fearful, and self-doubting. "Peter did not feel very brave; indeed, he felt he was going to be sick," wrote Lewis in *The Lion, the Witch, and the Wardrobe*. "But that made no difference to what he had to do. He rushed straight up to the monster and aimed a slash of sword at its side."[86]

As we'll see, the Christian faith of Tolkien and Lewis offered them a moral vantage point from which to grapple with the meaning of war. Their personal taste of combat, with all its troubling ambiguities, checked the impulse toward self-righteousness. Surely the daily routine of war, its moments of fear, boredom, exhaustion, hardship, and horror, saved them from ever romanticizing the experience. As Lewis wrote, many years after his wartime service:

> For let us make no mistake. All that we fear from all the kinds
> of adversity, severally, is collected together in the life of a soldier

on active service. Like sickness, it threatens pain and death. Like poverty, it threatens ill lodging, cold, heat, thirst, and hunger. Like slavery, it threatens toil, humiliation, injustice, and arbitrary rule. Like exile, it separates you from all you love.[87]

Nevertheless, belief in the existence of a moral order to the universe helped these authors to confront the human predicament: the diabolical and deeply rooted challenges to justice and peace in our world. Moreover, the inexpressible experience of war gave them a special empathy for the person who is asked to risk all for a noble cause. More often than not, their characters display an unexpected humility, a reticence about combat that can be overcome only by the prospect of a gathering storm of Evil.

Thus, in Tolkien's *The Lord of the Rings*, we follow Frodo Baggins in near-constant peril as he pursues his mission as a foot soldier in a great war. We see his fear as well as his determination to overcome it and remain true to his quest: "There is a seed of courage hidden (often deeply, it is true) in the heart of the fattest and most timid hobbit, waiting for some final and desperate danger to make it grow," Tolkien wrote. "He thought he had come to the end of his adventure, and a terrible end, but the thought hardened him. He found himself stiffening, as if for a final spring; he no longer felt limp like a helpless prey."[88]

CHAPTER 3

IN A HOLE IN THE GROUND THERE LIVED A HOBBIT

A few days before Second Lieutenant J. R. R. Tolkien set off for the Western Front in France, the greatest sea battle of the First World War began. On June 1, 1916, the British Grand Fleet challenged the German Navy in the North Sea. Known as the Battle of Jutland, a British force of twenty-eight battleships, nine battle cruisers, thirty-four light cruisers, and eighty destroyers clashed with twenty-four German battleships, five battle cruisers, eleven light cruisers, and sixty-three destroyers. It was a fearsome display of modern naval power.

British petty officer Ernest Francis, a gunner's mate aboard the battle cruiser *Queen Mary*, jumped overboard after his ship was blown out of the water. "I struck away from the ship as hard as I could and must have covered nearly fifty yards when there was a big smash," he wrote. "And coming behind me I heard a rush of water, which looked very like surf breaking on a beach and I realized it was the suction or backwash from the ship which had just gone."[1] The *Queen Mary* sank in ninety seconds, taking most of its thousand-man crew with her.

Given the casualties on both sides, there seemed to be no clear victor; citizens and soldiers alike were left wondering whether to celebrate a victory or mourn an inglorious defeat. "The one indisputable fact," said a nurse at a London hospital, "was that hundreds of young men, many of them midshipmen only just in their teens, had gone down without hope of rescue or under-standing of the issues to a cold, anonymous grave."[2] The losses were indeed devastating: a total of 6,097 British sailors perished at sea, compared to 2,551 Germans.

Among those caught up in the battle was Christopher Wiseman, a member of Tolkien's "Tea Club and Barrovian Society," or TCBS, a semi-secret society of friends who first met in 1911 at King Edward's School, Birmingham. Though others were included, its core members were Tolkien, Wiseman, Geoffrey Bache Smith, and Robert Gilson. All of them, with varying degrees of enthusi-asm, were drawn into the First World War as soldiers. Tolkien's circle shared a love of literature and a powerful desire to leave their mark on the world. Wiseman must have left his mark on Tolkien, because he named his son, Christopher, after him.

Before being sent off to war, members of the TCBS held a "Council" meeting at Wiseman's house in London, an exalted title borrowed, no doubt, from the diplomatic jargon of the day. They talked late into the night, sharing with one another their deepest convictions and aspirations. Given their evident loyalty to one another throughout the war years, they must have vowed to preserve their fellowship in whatever way they could. Tolkien later said it was at this moment that he first became aware of "the hopes and ambitions" that would propel him throughout his life.[3]

At about the same time that Tolkien enlisted in the British Expeditionary Force, Wiseman had joined the Navy and was assigned to the HMS *Superb*, part of the British Grand Fleet during the Battle of Jutland. He survived the encounter.

Meanwhile, the Germans staged another major assault at Verdun, a French outpost along the River Meuse, about 150 miles east of Paris. The Battle of Verdun—the longest battle of the war—had already been raging for fifteen weeks. Launched on February 21, 1916, it was an attempt to "bleed France white" by attacking a strategic fortress town and luring the French army into a fatal defensive. If successful, the assault would have knocked France out of the war and forced Britain to go it alone.

At the start of the battle, more than 140,000 German troops, supported by 1,200 artillery guns, began pounding French fortifications. The eight-mile sector of the German lines "erupted into a blaze of artillery the likes of which the world had never seen."[4] Woods were converted to stumps and craters. A French soldier described the scene thus: "Men were squashed. Cut in two or divided from top to bottom. Blown into showers; bellies turned inside out; skulls forced into the chest as if by a blow from a club."[5]

By the end of April, casualties at Verdun totaled 133,000 for the French and 120,000 for the Germans—with no end in sight. In the first week of June, the Germans turned their sights on Fort Vaux, and a savage fight for the outpost began. "It is maddening," wrote a French soldier. "One sees . . . a continuous cloud of smoke everywhere. Trees leap into the air like wisps of straw; it is an

unheard-of spectacle."[6] After a heroic defense, the French commander surrendered only because his men were literally dying of
thirst.[7] "Humanity is mad. It must be mad to do what it is doing,"
wrote a French lieutenant in his diary at Verdun. "Hell cannot be
so terrible."[8] The hellish campaign at Verdun would drag on until
December 1916.

LEAVING "THE LONELY ISLE"

News of these battles, of their ferocity and destructiveness,
was in the air as twenty-four-year-old Tolkien disembarked on
June 4, 1916. Trained as a battalion signals officer with the 11th
Lancashire Fusiliers, his preparation could hardly have equipped
him for the realities that lay ahead. He seemed to sense as much,
for he did not expect to return home alive. "Junior officers were
being killed off, a dozen a minute," Tolkien recalled. "Parting
from my wife then . . . it was like a death."[9]

As he crossed the English Channel, Tolkien gazed back at
his island home and turned his thoughts into poetry.[10] His short
poem, "The Lonely Isle," suggests his deep sadness as his familiar
world slipped further and further from sight:

> *Down the great wastes and in gloom apart*
> *I long for thee and thy fair citadel.*
> *Where echoing through the lighted elms at eve*
> *In a high inland tower there peals a bell:*
> *O lonely, sparkling isle, farewell![11]*

It is easy to imagine Tolkien, the untested soldier, drawing on this moment of separation when he described scenes of

parting in *The Lord of the Rings*. Recall Frodo's dark realization as he prepares to leave the Shire: "This would mean exile, a flight from danger to danger, drawing it after me. And I suppose I must go alone. . . . But I feel very small, and very uprooted, and well—desperate. The Enemy is so strong and terrible."[12]

As we've seen, there was an immense feeling of patriotic duty as Britain entered the conflict, a desire to "do one's bit" for King and Country. "I have implicit confidence in you, my soldiers," King George told the British Expeditionary Force in August 1914. "Duty is your watchword, and I know your duty will be nobly done."[13] Droves of men responded to the call with a kind of "intense, almost mystical patriotism."[14]

Relying on an all-volunteer military, Lord Kitchener, Secretary for War, initially called for another one hundred thousand men to bolster the regular army. But young men flooded recruitment offices so that by the spring of 1915 there were six hundred thousand additional men under arms. The *Birmingham Daily Post*, Tolkien's hometown paper, left no doubt about the obligation of the hour: "Patriotism insists that the unmarried shall offer themselves without thought or hesitation."[15] As Tolkien described the mood: "In those days, chaps signed up or were scorned publicly."[16]

Men enlisted together, forming "Pals' Battalions" drawn from their networks of families, friendships, and work relationships. "It is a story of a spontaneous and genuinely popular mass movement which has no counterpart in the modern, English-speaking world," writes John Keegan in *The Face of Battle*, "and perhaps could have none outside of its own time and place."[17]

At the beginning of 1916, there were nearly a million British troops on the Continent, and the number was increasing by about one hundred thousand every month. A. F. Winnington-Ingram,

Bishop of London, marveled at the "really astonishing" numbers of volunteers. "The revelation has been the outpouring of service both of men and women from the heart of a nation which its enemies thought was lost in comfort and wrapped in ignoble ease."[18] Yet Britain still relied on an all-volunteer army, and the numbers were insufficient to meet the demands of the war. Compared to the large continental armies of Germany and France, the British Expeditionary Force in early 1916 was still modest in size. German Kaiser Wilhelm II called the British army "contemptibly small."

Most importantly, twenty-two months of carnage had produced a military stalemate along the Western Front. The British government was determined to tilt the balance of forces. On January 27, 1916, Parliament passed the Military Service Act, introducing conscription to Britain for the first time. All men between the ages of eighteen and forty-one were required to enlist. "It was a nasty cleft to be in," Tolkien wrote many years later, "especially for a young man with too much imagination and little physical courage."[19]

LIFE AND DEATH IN THE TRENCHES

By the summer of 1916, the initial enthusiasm for war was fading. More than two hundred thousand British soldiers now lay dead, and another three hundred thousand wounded.[20] Soldiers kept on fighting—there was a remarkable loyalty among recruits of all ranks—but there was also a deepening sobriety, a grim determination to hold on. Abel Ferry lost not only his zeal for battle, but many of his cherished convictions: "Idealism is dupery," he wrote in 1916. "The world belongs to those who don't believe in ideas."[21] TCBS member Rob Gilson had joined the Cambridgeshire

Battalion as a second lieutenant. Like Tolkien, he was sent to the Western Front, where he encountered conditions previously unimaginable. "I could almost cry sometimes at the universal mud," he wrote, "and the utter impossibility of escaping from it."[22]

What Gilson described was the defining, iconic symbol of the war: the trench. For the typical British soldier, life in these elaborate ditches was a quagmire of cold, wet, rat-infested squalor. The trenches were deep enough to shelter a soldier and narrow enough to avoid direct hits from artillery fire. Every few yards a trench zigzagged, to limit the damage from mortar or machine-gun attacks. Trench walls, supported by sandbags, were in a constant state of decay. Trench floors, even if covered with wooden duckboards, filled up with water during heavy rains. "In two-and-a-half miles of trench which I waded yesterday," wrote Wilfred Owen to his mother, "there was not one inch of dry ground."[23]

Rats roamed about at will. Gorging themselves on human remains, some were the size of a cat. Disgusted and harassed by them, soldiers would shoot them, bayonet them, or club them to death. "We borrowed a large cat and shut it up at night to exterminate them, and found the place empty next morning," recorded a soldier in his diary. "The rats must have eaten it up, bones, fur, and all, and dragged it to their holes."[24]

As bad as the water, mud, rats, roaches, and lice was the smell: the stench of decaying flesh, human and animal, seemed to cover everything. Snipers, grenades, random shell fire, untreated wounds, disease—any number of causes made death, and the smell of death, a constant presence for soldiers on the front line. Writes historian John Keegan: "You could smell the front line miles before you could see it."[25]

The trenches provided the setting for much of the suffering

and lethality of the war. They formed a base of operations for each side's military, offering a measure of protection for soldiers and creating a demarcation line behind which the heavy guns were nested. "Millions of men for months occupied almost unchanging positions within close range of the enemy," explains historian Max Hastings in *Catastrophe 1914*. "Rigorous discipline became necessary to avoid exposing even an inch of flesh."[26]

During an assault, shells of death flew overhead in both directions, eventually finding their mark. "It exploded, and a cloud of black reek went up," wrote a British captain during an assault on a trench line. The explosion, he explained, threw up the earth and buried two or more soldiers alive. "You dug furiously. . . . At last you get them out, three dead, grey muddy masses, and one more jabbering live one. Then another shell falls and more are buried."[27]

No soldier, especially one with Tolkien's literary cast of mind, could ever forget the experience. As an undergraduate at Oxford, Tolkien already had discovered that he was drawn to ancient legends and the languages in which they were embedded. Not even the demands of active combat could completely distract him from his passion. He began writing bits and pieces of the legends that would form the basis of his epic trilogy: "The early work was mostly done in camps and hospitals between 1915 and 1918—when time allowed."[28]

Thus the battle scenes in *The Lord of the Rings* possess a grim authenticity. When Tolkien describes the Siege of Gondor—where the "fires leaped up" and "great engines crawled across the field" and the ground "was choked with wreck and with bodies of the slain"—he delivers the realism of the war veteran. "Busy as ants hurrying orcs were digging, digging lines of deep trenches in a huge ring, just out of bowshot from the walls," he wrote in *The Return of the King*. "And soon yet more companies of the enemy were swiftly setting up, each behind the cover of a trench, great engines for the casting of missiles."[29]

SLAUGHTER AT THE SOMME

In an effort to take pressure off the French forces and achieve a breakthrough in the conflict, the British conceived of a major offensive of their own, to begin in the summer of 1916. Winston Churchill, who had just returned to the Western Front as a battalion commander, warned the House of Commons against "futile offensives" that would kill thousands of young men overnight. Nevertheless, plans were drawn up for a renewed attack that would permanently alter Tolkien's life, and the lives of hundreds of thousands of English soldiers: the Battle of the Somme.

The weather on the morning of July 1, 1916, the first day of the Somme offensive, "was of the kind commonly called heavenly." Below, however, beginning at 7:00 a.m., British aircraft and artillery were raining down hell on German positions along the river. In just over an hour, nearly a quarter of a million shells—about thirty-five hundred shells a minute—were fired at the Germans. The roar was so loud that it was heard in North London, nearly two hundred miles away.

The British, in fact, had been pounding their targets for a week with heavy artillery. Soldiers were assured that this last burst of firepower would destroy what was left of the German wire, obliterate the deepest dugouts, and severely compromise German artillery power. Crossing No Man's Land, that dreadful death zone stretching between the opposing enemy trenches, would be a song. "You will be able to get over the top with a walking stick," one battalion was told, "you will not need rifles."[30]

At 7:30 a.m., to the sound of whistles, drums, and bagpipes, nearly one hundred thousand British troops climbed out of their trenches and attacked along the entire fourteen-mile front. They were confident of victory, even exuberant.

What they did not know was that the bombardment had not penetrated most of the German dugouts, or destroyed the wire, or knocked out the German heavy artillery. What they did not suspect was that they were "plodding forward across a featureless landscape to their own extermination."[31] Hundreds of German field guns and howitzers were turned on the advancing British troops, with devastating effect. "When we started to fire we just had to load and reload," said a German machine-gunner. "They went down in their hundreds. We didn't have to aim, we just fired into them."[32]

Before the sun sank beyond the grey banks of the River Somme, 19,420 British soldiers—Lloyd George called them "the choicest and best of our young manhood"—lay dead.[33] Most were killed in the first hour of the attack, many within the first minutes. Another 40,000 were wounded. Many battalions endured casualty rates (dead and wounded) of over 50 percent. Thus, July 1, 1916, the first day of the Battle of the Somme, marks the deadliest single day in British military history. "The agony of war took its toll on the Somme in full measure," writes Martin Gilbert in *The Somme*. "The heroism and horror of war were seen there without disguise, unembellished and unadorned."[34]

The Somme offensive would rage, inconclusively, until November 16—nearly five months of bloodletting that claimed more than 1.2 million dead and wounded. And to what end? "In offensive terms, the advance had achieved nothing," concludes

John Keegan. "Most of the dead were killed on ground the British held before the advance began."[35] Winston Churchill, who was on the front lines in 1916 as a lieutenant colonel, saw "a welter of slaughter" from beginning to end. "No strategic advantage of any kind had been gained."[36] One commanding officer reported stoically: "It was a magnificent display of trained and disciplined valor, and its assault only failed of success because dead men can advance no further."[37]

Among the dead was TCBS member Rob Gilson. Two nights before he was killed, Gilson had written home: "Guns firing at night are beautiful—if they were not so terrible. They have the grandeur of thunderstorms. But how one clutches at the glimpses of peaceful scenes. It would be wonderful to be a hundred miles from the firing line once again."[38]

Though he entered the war with great anxiety over his own capacities under the stress of battle, Gilson distinguished himself in his final moments. When his commanding officer was killed, Gilson took over and led his men "perfectly calmly and confidently" into No Man's Land.[39] His friend could not have been far from Tolkien's thoughts when, in *The Lord of the Rings*, he described as "curiously tough" the hobbits of the Shire. "They were, if it came to it, difficult to daunt or to kill; and they . . . could survive rough handling by grief, foe, or weather in a way that astonished those who did not know them well and looked no further than their bellies and their well-fed faces."[40]

INTO THE LINE

News of Gilson's death did not reach Tolkien for several weeks. As the battalion signals officer of the 11th Lancashire Fusiliers,

Tolkien's job was to maintain communication between the army staff directing the battle and the officers in the field. His tools included flares, signal lights, carrier pigeons, runners, and telephones. His was a vital link in the chain of command, since the information gathered in the field would direct artillery fire and deploy—or withdraw—troops as needed. Breakdowns in communication could cost hundreds, even thousands, of lives.

In the days before the Somme offensive, Tolkien and the eight hundred men of his Fusiliers unit were held back in a battle-ready support role, perhaps thirteen miles from the front. But on July 3, the third day of the battle, they headed for Bouzincourt, a village just three miles behind the line. Once they arrived, soldiers occupied every house, barn, cellar, and orchard.[41]

In an earlier war, the men would have been at a safe enough distance from the fighting to play a game of cricket. But not in this war with its new technologies of destruction. Chief among them was artillery, comprised of a wide variety of long-range weapons: field artillery, made up of 18-pounder guns and 4.5-inch howitzers, which could fire small shrapnel or high explosives to a range of six thousand yards; medium artillery, comprised of 60-pounder guns that could send explosive shells ten thousand yards; and trench mortars, which could lob four-inch bombs from one trench to another across No Man's Land.[42] Artillery carried the advantage not only of distance but of speed: thanks to hydraulic mechanisms and timing devices, the "shells" could be delivered to the enemy more rapidly, accurately, and for longer periods than anything ever seen in warfare. "For the first time in history, and from the beginning of the war to the end, artillery dominated," writes G. J. Meyer in *A World Undone*. "It did more killing between 1914 and 1918 than any other weapon."[43]

As Tolkien lay in a hut, probably reading letters from his wife, a German field gun bombarded the village. Tolkien, on the Western Front and caught up in one of the deadliest exchanges of the war, came under fire for the first time in his life.

How might the young soldier have drawn on this moment to describe the enormity of war in *The Lord of the Rings*? "This is no longer a bickering at the fords, raiding from Ithilien and from Anorien, ambushing and pillaging," says Beregond, a soldier in Gondor's army. "*This is a great war long planned, and we are but one piece in it, whatever pride may say.*"[44] Could this same moment have informed the anguish of Frodo Baggins after leaving the Shire and facing the Black Riders? "In that lonely place Frodo for the first time fully realized his homelessness and danger," Tolkien wrote. "He wished bitterly that his fortune had left him in the quiet and beloved Shire. He stared down at the hateful Road, leading back westward—to his home."[45]

Reflecting on his experiences years later, Tolkien acknowledged that his taste for fantasy was "quickened to full life by war" and that "the mythology (and associated languages) first began to take shape during the 1914–18 war."[46] Much of the "early parts" of his epic, he explained, were "done in grimy canteens, at lectures in cold fogs, in huts full of blasphemy and smut, or by candle light in bell-tents, *even some down in dugouts under shell fire.*"[47] In other words, Tolkien had begun to lay the foundation for his war trilogy.

The immediate challenge, though, was to stay alive. "Tolkien and his signalers were always vulnerable," explains Martin Gilbert. The village of Bouzincourt avoided much of the barrage, but wounded men from other areas of the front, many of them horribly mutilated, arrived by the hundreds. Members of Tolkien's battalion began digging graves.

Tolkien was especially anxious over the fate of two of his friends from the TCBS. He knew that Gilson was in the thick of the fighting on July 1, but nothing else. Nor did he know what had happened to Geoffrey Smith, another member of his inner circle. Remarkably, Smith appeared in Bouzincourt on July 6, alive and unharmed. Tolkien was overcome with joy, and the two met as often as they could amid the clamor of activity. They walked together in a field of poppies, strangely untouched by mortar fire, and talked about poetry, the war, and the future. The next day Smith's company, the Salford Pals, left for the trenches to support the British assault on Ovillers, a German stronghold.[48]

In *Tolkien and the Great War*, biographer John Garth describes the scene as Tolkien's turn for battle arrived on July 14, when his brigade was sent to reinforce the Ovillers campaign.[49] The night sky was flush with bursting shells and flares. Small wooden crosses dotted the landscape. Along the way they encountered many wounded taken from the battlefield. "So it was on the approach to Ovillers that Tolkien first encountered the lost of the Somme," Garth writes, "heralded by their stench, darkly hunched or prone, or hanging on the wire until a stab of brightness revealed them, the bloated and putrescent dead."[50]

The British line was a matrix of confusion and frustration. Phone lines running back to headquarters were easily tapped and could only be used as a last resort. Flags, flares, and lamps were also of limited use, since they attracted enemy fire. Most messages had to be sent by runners, who could be picked off by snipers. Thus, soldiers were effectively fighting in a "zone of mystery," with no sense of the enemy's movements or how to gain strategic advantage. "The job of the signaler was to shed some

light on the mystery by helping set up a battlefield communications system and using it," according to Garth. "In practice this
was an almost hopeless task."[51]

Worst of all was the scene in and around the trenches. The
bodies of dead soldiers lay everywhere: disfigured by shells, with
woeful eyes or faces blown off entirely. The wounded moaned or
wept with grief. Beyond the trenches, in No Man's Land, was a
landscape of lifeless desolation. Trees had been reduced to blackened sticks. The air was dense with smoke and the stench of
explosives and unburied corpses. Grass and crops had been swal-
lowed up by waves of mud.

After a heavy rain, it was commonplace to see the bodies of
soldiers lying facedown in pools or lakes of muddy water; once
injured, their sixty-pound packs sealed their fate. A young British
officer reported finding bodies of soldiers wounded on July 1 who
had "crawled into shell holes, wrapped their waterproof sheets
around them, taken out their Bibles and died like that."[52] War
correspondent Sir Philip Gibbs saw more than most. "Dead bodies were heaped there, buried and unburied," he wrote. "Men dug
into corruption when they tried to dig a trench. Men sat on dead
bodies when they peered through their periscopes. They ate and
slept with the stench of death in their nostrils."[53]

THE "ANIMAL HORROR" OF WAR

Just before midnight on July14, 1916, Tolkien and the Lancashire
Fusiliers were waiting in reserve as their comrades in the 7th
Brigade launched the next assault at Ovillers-la-Boisselle. They
were repelled. A second attack was planned for 2:00 a.m., and
this time Tolkien's battalion, with bayonets fixed, would lead it.

But enemy machine-gun fire and barbed wire thwarted their assault. The battalions fell back for the night.[54]

The next day they were at it again, exchanging bombs, hand grenades, and machine-gun fire with the enemy. The assault lasted all day. The ground, according to one survivor, was "torn up by shells and littered with dead bodies."[55] At sunset a white flag appeared at the German garrison at Ovillers: surrender. Tolkien, unharmed but physically and emotionally exhausted, had endured fifty hours of combat. Years later he described this period as "the animal horror of the life of active service."[56]

Upon returning to Bouzincourt, Tolkien found a terse and anxious note from G. B. Smith, explaining that Rob Gilson had been killed on the opening day of the Battle of the Somme. "Do please stick to me, you and Christopher," Smith wrote. "I am very tired and most frightfully depressed at this worst of news."[57] Smith turned his grief into poetry, and wrote a tribute to Gilson:

> Let us tell quiet stories of kind eyes
> And placid brows where peace and learning sate:
> Of misty gardens under evening skies
> Where four would walk of old, with steps
> sedate. . . .
>
> And draw nigh unto us for memory's sake,
>
> Because a look, a word, a deed, a friend,
> Are bound with cords that never a man may
> break,
> Unto his heart for ever, until the end.[58]

Writing to Smith, Tolkien described the love he felt for their fallen friend, "which I only realize now, more and more daily, that he has gone." Tolkien praised Gilson's "holiness of courage, suffering, and sacrifice." But he lamented the "bitter winnowing" of their number by the loss of their comrade. "I feel . . . immeasurably weaker and poorer now." King Edward's School in Birmingham, the birthplace of Tolkien's TCBS, held a minute of silence to honor the forty-two graduates killed in 1916. Among their sad roster was Robert Gilson. He was twenty-two years old.

"I do not know what is to be our move next or what is in store," Tolkien wrote to Smith. "Rumor is as busy as the universal weariness of all this war allows it to be. I wish I could know where you are."[59] With a friend dead, others missing, and a horrible battle raging around him, we can only imagine the condition of Tolkien's soul. Yet it brings to mind a moment in *The Lord of the Rings*, when Merry, cut off from the Fellowship, finds himself friendless and alone in the midst of their great quest. "Everyone he cared for had gone away into the gloom that hung over the distant eastern sky; and little hope at all was left in his heart that he would ever see any of them again."[60]

After just six days' rest in Bouzincourt, Tolkien was sent back into the line. From that point on, writes John Garth, "he lived almost constantly in a dugout."[61] The Fusiliers rehearsed for an attack on Regina Trench, the longest trench in the German line. Although it was of dubious strategic value, it already had cost the lives of many thousands of men. Canadian troops had seized and then lost a section of the trench. Another attack had failed, leaving many dead and wounded. Like so many other battles in the war, the campaign had become an ordeal of attrition.

Tolkien's battalion was ready to begin their attack on the

afternoon of October 19, 1916. But heavy rains delayed the assault for forty-eight hours. Weariness and anxiety were surely taking their toll on Tolkien and the Fusiliers as they imagined climbing out of their dugouts and into the blood and smoke and shelling of No Man's Land. "The fifteen minutes before 'going over' have a peculiar eeriness all their own," wrote a Scottish private. "As the zero hour approaches . . . we are left with nothing to take our minds off the dragging minutes."[62] Tolkien captured moments like this in *The Lord of the Rings*, where he most often seems to identify with the plight of the hobbits:

> Now he was one small soldier in a city preparing for a great assault, clad in the proud but somber manner of the Tower of the Guard. In some other time and place Pippin might have been pleased with his new array, but he knew now that he was taking part in no play; he was in deadly earnest the servant of a grim master in the greatest peril.[63]

What sustained Tolkien and his fellow soldiers? "The honor of my battalion and its opinion of me," wrote one officer. "These are now my sustaining motives in the game of war."[64] The resolve and discipline of British troops in the face of massive casualties during the battle remains one of the most remarkable facts of the First World War. "None could help thinking of what the next few hours would bring," wrote a soldier. "One minute's anguish and then, once in the ranks, faces became calm and serene, a kind of gravity falling upon them, while on each could be read the determination and expectation of victory."[65]

Finally, just after noon on October 21, the first two waves of infantrymen scrambled from their narrow trenches, followed by

Tolkien's signalers. Success: at 12:20 p.m., Tolkien, who was running the signals operation, told brigade headquarters that scores of Germans were surrendering. His division alone captured seven hundred German soldiers.

Yet their victory was not without cost: at least 41 Fusiliers were dead or missing, another 117 were wounded, many grievously. Many in Tolkien's division were cut down by their own artillery, casualties of the inescapable fog of war. Rev. Mervyn Evers, the battalion chaplain, appeared the next day, covered in blood. He had spent the entire night in No Man's Land, enduring German artillery fire and fierce cold, tending the wounded and comforting the dying.[66]

A week later Tolkien's battalion was on a train to Ypres, the scene of some of the most devastating battles of the war. Yet Tolkien was not with them; he was stricken with "trench fever," a bacterium that entered the bloodstream through lice. He was transported to an officers' hospital to recover. Chronic ill health sent him back to England on November 8, 1916, to recuperate at Birmingham University's wartime hospital.

A few weeks later, in December 1916, Tolkien received another sad letter, this time from Christopher Wiseman, his friend who survived the Battle of Jutland. In what should have been a safe zone, G. B. Smith was hit by a German shell fragment while walking along a road in the village of Souastre, north of Bouzincourt. An infection set in, and four days later he was dead.

It was a grievous blow. Smith had begun to write poetry during the war and shared it with Tolkien whenever he could. To honor his friend's memory, Tolkien edited a collection of his poems after the war and published them under the title *Spring Harvest*. In the foreword to the book, Tolkien noted that poems such as "The Burial of Sophocles" were written under fire: "The final version was sent to me from the trenches." Shortly before his death, Smith had written to Tolkien with a sense of foreboding: "May God bless you, my dear John Ronald, and may you say the things I have tried to say so long after I am not there to say them, if such be my lot."[67]

A VISION OF MORDOR

Mostly confined to a sickbed in England, Tolkien faced a grim accounting. Gilson and Smith were dead. So was Ralph Stuart Payton, another member of the TCBS. He, too, had fought at the Somme. He was killed in action on July 22, 1916, his body never identified. Gone also was Thomas Kenneth "Tea Cake" Barnsley, who was in the debating society with Tolkien. He served as a captain in the 1st Birmingham Battalion, was buried alive by a trench mortar, escaped—only to be killed in action near Ypres in June 1917.

Trench fever probably spared Tolkien's life. The 11th Lancashire Fusiliers went back into action on May 27, 1918, near the River Aisne, and sustained enormous casualties. The entire battalion was presumed dead or taken prisoner.

Still recovering from his illness, Tolkien was nevertheless strong enough to begin sketching out the foundation for his epic story. He of course retained his love of medieval literature, especially the themes of beauty and mortality in works such as *Beowulf*. Years later, in his groundbreaking essay, "On Translating Beowulf," Tolkien offered an insight into the poignant vision of the work that so absorbed him: "The poet who spoke these words saw in his thought the brave men of old walking under the vault of heaven upon the island earth beleaguered by the Shoreless Seas and the outer darkness, enduring with stern courage the brief days of life, until the hour of fate when all things should perish."[68]

Whatever else informed Tolkien's literary vision, we cannot overlook the backdrop of war: the life-and-death struggle that harasses every front-line soldier, the "animal horror" of trench warfare, the staggering desolation of No Man's Land.[69] The scenes at the Battle of the Somme, especially the early days of slaughter and futility, could not fail to leave their mark on the human conscience. Might Tolkien have had in mind his comrades, those who fell at the Somme, when he described the Siege of Gondor in *The Lord of the Rings*?

> Yet their Captain cared not greatly what they did or how many might be slain: their purpose was only to test the strength of the defense and to keep the men of Gondor busy in many places. All before the walls on either side of the Gate the ground was choked with wreck and with bodies of the slain; yet still driven as by a madness more and more came up.[70]

Indeed, it would be remarkable if the destruction Tolkien witnessed along the Western Front did not find expression in his creative works. "The horror of these landscapes is that they are not naturally produced but are a product of man's destructive misuse of technology," writes Nancy Marie Ott. "Battlefields like this simply did not exist before World War I."[71]

Thus on the desolate path to Mordor we encounter "dead grasses and rotting reeds" that "loomed up in the mists like ragged shadows of long-forgotten summers."[72] We see "a land defiled, diseased beyond healing."[73] We watch Sam Gamgee, during the passage through the marshes, catch his foot and fall on his hands, "which sank deep into sticky ooze, so that his face was brought close to the surface of the dark mire." Looking intently into the glazed and grimy muck, he is startled by what he finally sees. "There are dead things, dead faces in the water," he said with horror. "Dead faces!" Gollum laughed. "The Dead Marshes, yes, yes: that is their name," he cackled.[74]

War historian Martin Gilbert, in a chance interview with Tolkien at Oxford in the 1960s, spoke with him about his experience at the Battle of the Somme. "Tolkien remembered, as vividly as if it were yesterday, the constant danger of German artillery shells, ranging throughout the area, falling with their screech and roar, and clouds of earth and mud, and the fearful cries of men who had been hit."[75] Gilbert, who wrote a definitive account of the Somme offensive, noted that Tolkien's description of the Dead Marshes matches precisely the macabre experience of the soldiers in that battle: "Many soldiers on the Somme had been confronted by corpses, often decaying in the mud, that had lain undisturbed, except by the bombardment, for days, weeks and even months."[76]

In a letter to L. W. Forster, written in December 1960, Tolkien confirmed the influence of the war on his story, at least in his description of its bleak landscapes: "The Dead Marshes and the approaches to the Morannon owe something to Northern France after the Battle of the Somme."[77]

THE COURAGE OF "QUITE SMALL PEOPLE"

Not all Tolkien's war experiences, however, produced such dark narratives. In a letter to W. H. Auden, he explained how the idea for *The Hobbit*—the prequel to *The Lord of the Rings*—first came into his mind. It happened years after the war, after he had become Professor of Anglo-Saxon at Oxford University, while he was sitting and grading student papers. "On a blank leaf I scrawled: 'In a hole in the ground there lived a hobbit.' I did not and do not know why. . . . Names always generate a story in my mind. Eventually I thought I'd better find out what hobbits were like."[78]

We don't know why Tolkien wrote those enigmatic words. But we do know what hobbits are like: from his own account, the character of the hobbit was a reflection of the ordinary soldier, steadfast in his duties while suffering in that dreary "hole in the ground," the front-line trench.

Most of the members of the British Expeditionary Force were "citizen soldiers," drawn largely from the working classes. Unlike the French, Italian, Russian, and German armies, the BEF did not experience a large-scale collapse in discipline or morale.[79] Even during the most intensive campaigns along the Western Front, they showed a "remarkable resilience" relative to other armies.[80] The change in character that comes over Sam Gamgee was probably not unlike the transformation that Tolkien must have witnessed among many of his fellow soldiers in battle: "But even as hope died in Sam, or seemed to die, it was turned to a new strength. Sam's plain hobbit-face grew stern, almost grim, as the will hardened in him, and he felt through all his limbs a thrill, as if he was turning into some creature of stone and steel that neither despair nor weariness nor endless barren miles could subdue."[81]

If this was the character of the British soldier in the Great War, then it explains the admiration of Tolkien and many others over the years. As John Keegan concludes in *The Face of Battle*: "The British Expeditionary Force of 1916 was one of the most remarkable and admirable military formations ever to have taken the field."[82] In his magisterial work, *The World Crisis*, Winston Churchill extolled the qualities of the British army with his usual eloquence: "Unconquerable except by death . . . they set up a monument of native virtue which will command the wonder, the reverence and the gratitude of our island people as long as we endure as a nation among men."[83] Even Sir Philip Gibbs, who became severely critical of military leadership, confessed his astonishment at the valor of British troops, praising the "individual courage beyond the normal laws of human nature as I thought I knew them once."[84]

Historians still debate the ultimate achievement of these soldiers, and the causes for which they fought. Were they merely fodder for a vast and merciless military machine that ravaged Europe to no good end? Or did they play a vital role in halting German aggression and preventing the dominance of a brutal and oppressive juggernaut over the Continent? Whatever Tolkien thought about these questions, he was careful never to demean the significance of the soldier at his post: "I have always been impressed that we are here, surviving, because of the indomitable courage of quite small people against impossible odds." The hobbits were made small, he explained, "to show up, in creatures of very small physical power, the amazing and unexpected heroism of ordinary men 'at a pinch.' "[85]

Tolkien the soldier lived among these "ordinary men," fought alongside them, witnessed their courage under fire, joked with them, mourned with them, and watched them die. Thus the "small people" who fought and suffered in the Great War helped inspire the creation of the unlikely heroes in Tolkien's greatest imaginative work. Like the soldiers in that war, the homely hobbits could not have perceived how the fate of nations depended upon their stubborn devotion to duty.

Perhaps this was Tolkien's quiet way of suggesting that we may, in the end, owe more to these forgotten dead than our modern temperament allows. "That is a chapter of ancient history which it might be good to recall," advises Gandalf in *The Fellowship of the Ring*. "For there was sorrow then too, and gathering dark, but great valor, and great deeds that are not wholly vain."[86]

CHAPTER 4

THE LION, THE
WITCH, AND THE WAR

On September 30, 1914, barely a month after British troops were deployed to the Western Front, C. S. Lewis wrote his father from Great Bookham. Lewis had just arrived to study the classics with his father's former tutor, William Thompson Kirkpatrick, and he was dumbstruck by the beauty of an English village seemingly unmolested by time. Yet the mood of "perfect restfulness" that Lewis first observed upon his arrival was slipping away.[1]

England had hoped to remain out of the war, but the Kaiser's decision on August 4 to send German troops through Belgium compelled Britain to intervene. The British prime minister declared war on Germany the same day, and military recruitment campaigns were immediately launched around the country. Posters delivered the message: "Men of the Empire to Arms! God

Save the King!" "If England Falls You Fall!" "The Empire Needs Men!" and "It is Nice in the Surf but What About the Men in the Trenches? Go and Help." Thus Lewis wrote: "There is a good deal of war fever raging here, as is natural."[2]

There would be a good deal more in the weeks and months ahead. British troops could not prevent a German takeover of the last stronghold of the Belgian army, the strategic port city of Antwerp. By October 6, round-the-clock German shelling sent sixty thousand Belgian troops fleeing the city. Soon thousands of refugees arrived in England, and in Great Bookham there were plans to take them in. Wrote Lewis to his father: "Everyone at Bookham is engaged in a conspiracy for 'getting up' a cottage for Belgian refugees."

Meanwhile, German submarines were operating in the Irish Sea, posing a threat to civilian travel. "There is the frightful prospect of living on opposite sides of the channel for two, five, or six years," Lewis complained. "That of course is unthinkable."[3] Talk of German spies was rampant.

Soldiers on leave, many bearing the wounds of battle, were returning to England with grim stories of combat. A former student of Kirkpatrick's, Oswald Smythe, arrived at Kirkpatrick's house in March 1915 and made an impression on Lewis for his courage: "That Gerald Smythe of whom I told you, who lost an arm in the war, was staying with us last week. He is really wonderful: he has only been out of bed about a month and is going back to the front again next week. It does one good to see a person thoroughly cheerful under circumstances like this, and actually eager to be there again."[4]

Lewis did not share Smythe's eagerness for battle, however. Perhaps his reading of Homer's *The Iliad*, which he had begun a few weeks after the war broke out, had something to do with it. Although there is a notion that some British officers went into battle with *The Iliad* in their backpacks and the rage of Achilles in their hearts, Lewis was not one of them.[5] Whatever elements of battle glory there are in *The Iliad* are more than offset by its scenes of suffering. As Bernard Knox observes in his introduction to the work, the men in Homer's war story die in agony: they drop to their knees screaming, clawing the ground, moaning and gasping for life. "And death is the end," writes Knox. "Homer offers no comforting vision of life beyond the grave."[6]

Conversations with his older brother, Warren ("Warnie"), already a second lieutenant with the British Expeditionary Force, would have been equally sobering. Serving on the Western Front since November 1914, Warnie had seen enough slaughter for a lifetime. "I shall never be able to forget—a boy lay asleep on a bank and the mess by his head was his brains."[7] Not long after a visit with his brother, on leave in July 1915, Lewis noted in a diary that he "had ghastly dreams about the front and getting wounded last night."[8]

In any event, Lewis was focused on his academic career; he wanted to explore his love of the classics and English literature and to cultivate friendships with like-minded scholars. Having been born in Belfast, Northern Ireland, Lewis was still exempt from service in the British military. Not yet eighteen years old, he could not enlist—nor did he wish to. "Apropos of conscription, I sincerely hope that one of two things may happen," he wrote his father. "Either that the war may be over before I am eighteen, or that conscription may not come into force before I have volunteered. I shouldn't fancy going out to meet the others—as a conscript."[9]

A TASTE OF GOODNESS

In the meantime, Lewis devoted himself to the reading of good books, especially the Romantics, including the works of William Morris, John Keats, and Percy Shelley. He found himself, by his own description, "waist deep in Romanticism." With news of soldiers perishing each week by the thousands at Verdun, Lewis was also reaching for works that would nourish a growing taste for fantasy. In March 1916, while waiting for a train at Great Bookham Station, Lewis bought a copy of George MacDonald's *Phantastes: A Faerie Romance*, a book that would reach deeply and unexpectedly into his imagination. Writing to his friend Arthur Greeves, he described a "great literary experience" in discovering the work. "Whatever the book you are reading now, you simply MUST get this at once."

What is the quality in MacDonald's story that Lewis found so compelling? MacDonald, a one-time Scottish minister, was a nineteenth-century author of fantasy novels. Regarded as among his most important works, *Phantastes* explores what at first seems to be a man's search for feminine beauty, but turns out to be a quest for something much more profound, something deeply spiritual. Lewis later described its effect on him this way:

> The whole book had about it a sort of cool, morning innocence, and also, quite unmistakably, a certain quality of Death, *good* Death. What it actually did to me was to convert, even to baptize (that was where the death came in) my imagination. It did nothing to my intellect nor (at that time) to my conscience. Their turn came far later and with the help of many other books and men.[10]

What does it mean to have one's imagination "converted" or "baptized" by a work of fantasy? In Lewis's case, it seems that *Phantastes* rescued his imaginative cast of mind from its dark tendencies—made darker, perhaps, by the onset of the war—and introduced him to a "bright shadow," a voice or force that drew him out of himself. It set before him a vision of a world that must have seemed wholly unlike his own: pure and radiant, yet morally severe.

Perhaps this was MacDonald's intent. In his essay "The Fantastic Imagination," MacDonald hinted at one of his objectives in using the genre of the fairy tale. "The best thing you can do for your fellow, next to rousing his conscience, is—not to give him things to think about, but to wake things up that are in him; or say, to make him think things for himself."[11] Something, it seems, was awakened within Lewis, something that other authors had failed to summon. After the war, in a diary entry in 1923, Lewis hinted at the enormous importance he attached to the book: "After this I read Macdonald's *Phantastes* over my tea, which I have read many times and which I really believe fills for me the place of a devotional book."[12]

Lewis's brother, Warnie, with whom he shared a close and lifelong friendship, called his discovery of MacDonald "a turning point in his life."[13] Biographers Roger Green and Walter Hooper regard the work as "the highlight among Lewis's literary discoveries" during this time.[14] Nearly forty years later, Lewis was still recommending MacDonald's work to friends and acquaintances.[15] Biographer George Sayer draws special attention to the book and the enduring power of its symbolism. "The influence of *Phantastes* on Jack lasted many years, perhaps all his life," he writes. "It had a transforming influence on his attitude toward the ordinary, common things around him, imbuing them with its own spiritual quality."[16]

A GATHERING STORM

That may be so in the long run, but the transformation described showed little sign of spilling over into Lewis's exterior life. His letters during this period, when touching on matters of faith, were generally skeptical.

Lewis was also dismissive of the war, perhaps his way of putting its deadly prospect out of his mind. In a letter to Arthur Greeves in June 1915, he described "the prettiest girl I have ever seen in my life." She reminded Lewis of a beloved portion of Franz Liszt's *Hungarian Rhapsody* No. 1. "If you will play that record over, trying to turn that music into a person, you will know just how she looked and talked. Just 18, and off to do some ridiculous war-work, nursing or something like that at Dover of all places—what a shame!"[17]

In a letter to his father, Lewis continued to speculate that peace would arrive before he was forced to make a decision about enlistment: "I think we may reasonably hope that the war will be over before it begins to concern me personally."[18] Such hopes, however, were already proving futile.

On June 15, German zeppelins attacked London, hitting the busy Waterloo Station. The action, aimed at terrorizing civilians, helped to harden public animosity against Germany. "The Zeppelins over Scarborough and London were harbingers of a new era in which death would rain down from the sky on defenseless town-dwellers," writes historian Niall Ferguson.[19] Lewis, staying at the Kirkpatrick home, could see electric flashes in the skies caused by the bomb explosions. If the wind was blowing just right, he could "hear the mutter and grumble of the far distant guns in France."[20]

A year later the war was mired in stalemate. Conscription, which went into effect in January 1916, made Lewis's decision for him. He could not remain behind while other men his age were sent to the front; he resigned himself to the prospect of enlisting.

"It makes me so sad to think I shall have only two more sets of holidays of the good old type," he wrote, "for in November comes my 18th birthday, military age, and the 'vasty fields' of France, which I have no ambition to face."[21] Lewis wrote about a school friend, Donald Hardman, who was to be drafted into the military by Christmas. "He . . . wants to know what I am going to do. . . . Of course if it turned out to be convenient, I should like to have a friend with me in the army, but it is hardly worth while making any special provisions for so small a matter. We shall see how it all works out."[22]

On June 30, 1916—on the eve of the Battle of the Somme—Lewis wrote to his father expressing relief at the news that his father's nephew, Richard Lewis, had been "safely wounded" in France and thus taken out of harm's way. "It is by far the best thing that can happen to a man in the trenches."

He was right, of course. Historians estimate that perhaps a third of all Allied casualties on the Western Front occurred in the trenches, either from enemy fire or disease. With twelve thousand miles of trenches on the Allied side alone, stretching from Flanders to the Swiss Alps, it is not hard to understand the death toll. Lewis mused that the "really unlucky ones" may serve without injury for a year or more—"always it would seem in the long run to be killed after returning from a leave." The touch of fatalism is understandable, given the notorious depredations of trench warfare.

Indeed, in the same letter Lewis sensed that the war was entering a new phase of suffering: "Things look pretty black at present, don't they?"[23] The next day, on July 1, things were to become exponentially darker, as British and French troops launched the Somme offensive, a frenzy of concentrated killing that had almost no historical precedent in the annals of warfare.

THE CASE AGAINST GOD

Two weeks later, on July 14, as Tolkien and his men were preparing for their campaign at Ovillers, Lewis wrote to his father about "big news from the front" involving the Ulster Volunteer Force. The Irish soldiers, by their dedication and heroism in battle, compelled the War Department to accept them as an integral part of the British Army. "I suppose the losses are felt very heavily in Belfast: here, nobody seems to have noticed anything."[24]

The losses Lewis had in mind were those sustained by the 36th Ulster Division on the first day of the Somme offensive. The Ulstermen had captured the Schwaben Redoubt, a German stronghold with a fortified bunker more than twenty feet deep. But by nightfall the Germans had driven them back, and many were caught between the Germans and their own artillery. At least two thousand Ulstermen—more than a tenth of all the British fatalities on July 1—died in the firefight.[25]

Nevertheless, their courage earned them high honors. Four Victoria Crosses were awarded to men of the Ulster Division for their bravery on that opening day of the campaign. The first Victoria Cross of the Battle of the Somme was given to William

McFadzean, from Belfast, who saved the lives of fellow soldiers by throwing his body onto two bombs tossed into a trench.

What effect was news of the war having on Lewis? It is hard to say. Many years later, speaking to another generation of young men caught up in a great war, Lewis insisted that war produced at least one benefit: it forced us to consider our own mortality. "If active service does not prepare a man for death," he asked, "what conceivable concentration of circumstances would?"[26] There is little sign in the summer of 1916, however, that he was intellectually preparing himself for anything other than an academic career.

A deepening atheism may have had something to do with it. Lewis was reared in the Anglican Church, but he came to associate Christianity with "ugly architecture, ugly music, and bad poetry." Church sermons seemed vapid and irrelevant.

Lewis's doubts about God and Christianity were reinforced by his tutor, Kirkpatrick, under whom he studied before applying to Oxford. Kirkpatrick was, in Lewis's words, "a hard, satirical atheist." From Kirkpatrick Lewis learned that unexamined beliefs and assumptions must be taken to the woodshed. Hardly any subject was taboo, including the war, which had begun just weeks before Lewis came under Kirkpatrick's tutelage. "The commonest metaphors would be questioned," Lewis recalled, "till some bitter truth had been forced from its hiding place."

Thus a typical early exchange:

L: "These fiendish German atrocities—"
K: "But are not fiends a figment of the imagination?"
L: "Very well, then; these brutish atrocities—"
K: "But none of the brutes does anything of the kind!"

L: "Well, what am I to call them?"

K: "Is it not plain that we must call them simply
Human?"[27]

Kirkpatrick's ruthless rationality—like "red beef and strong beer"—exerted an enduring influence on his student. Lewis embraced the necessity of logic and reason, even as he pursued literary Romanticism. He learned not to abandon his conclusions, especially about spiritual matters, just because they might be unpopular. Shortly after the war, upon hearing of Kirkpatrick's death, Lewis recalled the enormous impact of his mentor on his life. "It is however no sentiment, but plainest fact to say that I at least owe him in the intellectual sphere as much as one human being can owe another," he wrote to his father. "It was an atmosphere of unrelenting clearness and rigid honesty of thought that one breathed from living with him—and this I shall be the better for as long as I live."[28]

Nevertheless, in a series of letters to Arthur Greeves, Lewis defended his atheism with arguments that were perfectly in sync with the intellectual fashions of his day. "You ask me my religious view: you know, I think, that I believe in no religion," he wrote. "There is absolutely no proof for any of them, and from a philosophical standpoint Christianity is not even the best."[29]

Emerging academic disciplines such as psychology and sociology explained the rise of Christianity and other belief systems as primitive man's attempt to cope with a frightening and dangerous world. Thus, for Lewis, Christianity was "one mythology among many"—and as false as all the others. "All religions, that is, all mythologies to give them their proper name are merely man's own invention—Christ as much as Loki." Great men came to be regarded by their followers as gods, Lewis explained, around whom a cult emerged. "Now all this you must have heard before," he wrote. "It is the recognized scientific account of the growth of religions."[30]

He advised Greeves to direct his own intellectual questions into the study of philosophy: "Its probings would at least save you from the intellectual stagnation that usually awaits a man who has found complete satisfaction in some traditional religious system."[31] If Lewis considered himself an atheist, he was a soft atheist; he would not completely rule out the possibility of something existing outside the material world. He admitted that "the universe is an absolute mystery," and that new discoveries about the world should be expected and welcomed. "In the meantime," he wrote, "I am not going to go back to the bondage of believing in any old (and already decaying) superstition."

When Lewis personally encountered the "unskilled butchery of the first German war," the attempt to reconcile a loving God with the problem of suffering appeared futile.[32] As we'll explore later, Lewis would write a series of poems, called *Spirits in Bondage*, expressing his distress over the failure of religious belief. The burden of belief, especially in wartime, would become intolerable.

A "TREATY WITH REALITY"

A more immediate burden, however, was now upon him. Just as Tolkien's military career was drawing to a close, Lewis enlisted in the British Expeditionary Force. In December 1916 he won a scholarship to University College, Oxford, and hoping to secure an officer's commission, joined the Officers' Training Corps.

When Lewis arrived at Oxford on April 16, 1917, he found the university cluttered with a "huge mass of military people." Wounded soldiers, cared for by a staff of nurses, occupied an entire quad of the college.[33] The cadets training for commissions were "a rather bad lot," Lewis complained, and are "busily engaged in eating and drinking on their splendid pay, for tomorrow they die."[34] Most everyone else was off to war.

Lewis endeavored to put the war out of his mind until the day he deployed for France. In a May 27 letter to Greeves, he bad-mouthed a "priggish, illiterate" freshman for talking incessantly of his brother and cousin who had been killed at the front. "Well of course I respect them for it, and I sympathize with him for losing them. At the same time, I don't think they need be dragged into every single conversation, on every opportunity!"[35]

Years later, recalling this period in his life, Lewis admitted that he "put the war on one side to a degree which some people will think shameful and some incredible." He denied, though, that he was trying to evade reality. "I maintain that it was rather a treaty with reality," he wrote, "the fixing of a frontier." It seems that Lewis made a pact with his country that left him at least partially in control: "You shall have me on a certain date, not before. I will die in your wars if need be, but till then I shall live my own life. You may have my body, but not my mind."[36] Based on his letters to friends and family, he appeared to keep up his end of the treaty.

Almost immediately, Lewis began training for trench warfare. "We spend a good deal of time in 'the trenches,' " he wrote to his father. He described the model trenches assembled on campus grounds, complete with dugouts, shell holes, and graves. "This last touch of realistic scenery," he quipped, "seems rather superfluous."[37]

He was then sent across Oxford to Keble College, where he spent his days "trench digging and route marching under a blazing sun."[38]

Nevertheless, little of the training Lewis received could prepare him for what he would encounter in combat: the mortars, machine guns, grenades, gas, or barbed wire. "All you do is lead your party onto parade, hand them over to their instructor, and then walk about doing nothing at all," he wrote. "It is a little tiring to the legs and I think will finally result in atrophy of the brain."[39]

During his training Lewis became friends with two men who would have a profound effect on his life. One was Edward Francis "Paddy" Moore, an Irishman from Bristol—"quite a good fellow"—with whom he shared a room at university. The other was Laurence Bertrand Johnson, elected a scholar of Queen's College, Oxford, whom Lewis admired for his intellect and literary tastes. "I think the only real change that you will find in me is an increasing tendency towards philosophy," he wrote Greeves, "which has grown in the course of many interesting talks with my good friend Johnson."[40]

THE ATHEIST IN A FOXHOLE

After three years of living with the knowledge of war, Lewis was ordered to deploy for France. He was commissioned as a second lieutenant in the Somerset Light Infantry, a combat regiment. On November 17, 1917, he sailed from Southampton to Le Havre in Normandy, expecting to undergo more training. Instead, twelve days later, he was sent to the front line. He arrived on his nineteenth birthday.

Writing from a village close to the town of Arras, Lewis concealed from his father the potential danger. "I suppose we have no reason to grumble: this was bound to come sooner or later. There is no need to worry for a good time yet, and I'll try and let you hear every day when there is."[41] Months later, Lewis would continue to shield his father from the truth of the trenches. "You will be anxious to hear my first impressions of trench life," he wrote. "This is a very quiet part of the line and the dug outs are very much more comfortable than one imagines at home."[42]

In fact, Lewis's company spent much of the bitter winter months in the trenches near Monchy-Le-Preux, a scene of intense fighting and destruction. The Germans were driven out of the village, but reestablished their trench line about five hundred yards east, roughly a stone's throw from the British line.[43] On the day Lewis arrived, November 29, there was "considerable enemy shelling." On the following day, his first day in the line, the enemy "shelled the trenches heavily practically all day." A captain in his regiment was wounded.[44]

"Through the winter," Lewis wrote, "weariness and water were our chief enemies."[45] Lewis learned to sleep while marching. He knew the feeling of ice-cold water filling up his boot when it struck hidden barbed wire. He encountered "the very old and the very recent dead" on the battlefield.[46] His experiences at Monchy-Le-Preux prompted Lewis to write a handful of poems about the war. In "French Nocturne," he echoed the sense of dehumanization expressed by many war veterans:

> Long leagues on either hand the trenches spread
> And all is still; now even this gross line
> Drinks in the frosty silences divine
> The pale, green moon is riding overhead. . . .

What call have I to dream of anything?

I am a wolf. Back to the world again,
And speech of fellow-brutes that once were men
Our throats can bark for slaughter: cannot sing.[47]

Biographer Alister McGrath believes that the merciless slaughter of war sharpened Lewis's doubts about God. "His wartime experiences reinforced his atheism," McGrath writes. "His poetry of the period rails against the silent, uncaring heaven."[48] Although we cannot know for certain, it does seem that the shock of mortal combat stirred a fresh revulsion for the pious doctrines of his youth. In "De Profundis," Lewis scorned the notion of a loving God who intervenes in human affairs:

Come let us curse our Master ere we die,
For all our hopes in endless ruin lie.
The good is dead. Let us curse God most High.[49]

Lewis escaped the "endless ruin" of war, temporarily at least, when he contracted trench fever and was removed from the front. In February 1918 he was sent to No. 10 British Red Cross Hospital at Le Tréport, near the French coast. He immediately wrote his friend Arthur Greeves: "Here I am safely ensconced in a bed in hospital, miles away from the line, thank the gods, and therefore at last in a position to write you a more or less respectable letter." It is hard to overstate the sense of relief that soldiers like Tolkien and Lewis experienced once they were taken out of harm's way. Max Plowman, who survived the Battle of the Somme, wrote that to be safely out of the trenches "is like being born again."[50] Lewis called his hospital stay "an unmixed blessing.[51]

The blessing would not endure. Instead, after recovering, Lewis was rushed back to the front. "We have just come back from a four days tour in the front line during which I had about as many hours sleep," he wrote his father on March 5. "Then . . . we spent the whole night digging."[52] Two weeks later, on March 19, Lewis and his battalion arrived at Fampoux, near Arras, and began preparations for a major assault.

"THIS IS WHAT HOMER WROTE ABOUT"

March 1918, in fact, was a moment of supreme danger for the Allies. The Communist Revolution in November 1917 had thrown Russia, a member of the Allied forces, into chaos. The Brest-Litovsk Treaty, signed on March 3, 1918, took Russia out of the war—a potential disaster for the Allied cause. With Russia neutralized, Germany no longer needed to fight a war on two fronts: she could drive the British from the Somme and the French from the Aisne and achieve total victory on the Western Front. The German railway system began moving divisions from the Eastern Front westward into France, along with hundreds of heavy guns and machine guns. The Central Powers were preparing to launch a massive spring offensive, their "last great onslaught."

The German attack commenced on March 21, with an artillery bombardment that lasted five hours. At least 6,000 German heavy guns, 3,000 mortars, 326 fighter aircraft, and hundreds of tons of mustard gas were hurled against the British lines. On the first day of the battle the Germans advanced more than four miles, taking 21,000 soldiers prisoner. Winston Churchill, visiting a front-line headquarters when the shelling began, barely escaped with his life.

Great Britain was sending thirty thousand troops a day into France, but they were not enough; the Allied effort was collapsing. "We cannot keep our divisions supplied with drafts for more than a short time at the present rate of loss," British prime minister Lloyd George warned his ambassador in Washington DC. "This situation is undoubtedly critical and if America delays now she may be too late."[53]

Under President Wilson, the United States had declared war on Germany on April 6, 1917, promising the Allies hundreds of thousands of fresh recruits. But it took nearly a year before US "doughboys" began arriving in France. Although the Americans still lacked sufficient numbers to form their own brigades, Wilson gave the green light for US troops to join their British and French counterparts on the Western Front. Beginning on March 23, 1918, roughly a million American troops would arrive over the next six months. My grandfather, Michele Loconte, in the 91st Division of the First American Army, was among their ranks.

On March 24, the day after Wilson's order, Germany crossed the River Somme, threatening to drive a wedge between the British and French armies. The German offensive would eventually be thwarted, but at a terrible cost.[54]

Among the casualties in the opening days of the battle was Edward "Paddy" Moore, second lieutenant with the 2nd Battalion of the Rifle Brigade and Lewis's friend from his Oxford days. Moore was last seen on March 24, defending a position against a much larger German force. Lewis had forged a close bond with Moore, his sister, and their mother, Mrs. Janie King Moore. Lewis and Moore promised each other that if either one of them was killed, the other would care for his surviving parent—a promise that Lewis kept.

Mrs. Moore wrote to Albert Lewis months later, after she finally learned of her son's death: "They tell me he was taken a prisoner, overthrew his guards, got back to our lines to be sent over again . . . was shot through the head and killed instantaneously," she wrote. "I had built up such hopes on my only son, and they are buried with so many others in that wretched Somme."[55]

Albert Lewis was especially anxious about his own son's situation; he had hoped, in vain, to get Lewis reassigned to safer duty on the front. On April 8, Lewis dashed off a note to tell his father he was safe. "We have had a fairly rough time, though we were not really in the thick of it," he wrote. "I have lost one or two of my best friends and in particular a fellow called Perrett who used to be at Malvern, and who got a bit in the eye."[56] Frank Winter Perrett was in the 1st Battalion of the Somerset Light Infantry when he was wounded on March 29. He survived his injuries.

On April 14, the Somerset Light Infantry began their own assault on the German-held village of Riez du Vinage, near Arras. Knowledge of a previous battle must have been on their minds. Almost exactly a year earlier, in April 1917, the Allies had staged a large offensive, the Battle of Arras, which drew troops from the four corners of the British Empire.[57] It was to be "the knockout blow" on the Western Front. Instead, it was an ambiguous bloodbath. When the assault was finally called off, it had cost the British and French 450,000 casualties, dead and wounded.

A year later, Britain's military leadership was no less determined to fight the German foe to the death. It was widely believed that a German victory on the Western Front now would be the end of the Allied cause. Lieutenant General Sir Douglas Haig, commander of the British forces in Europe, had just issued the order: "Every position must be held to the last man. There must be no retirement. With our backs to the wall and believing in the justice of our cause, each man must fight to the end."[58]

At 6:30 p.m., as British artillery laid down a barrage, the Somerset Light Infantry went into action. They met intense machine-gun fire. "Owing to the accuracy of this fire," according to the battalion report, "the advance was temporarily held up."[59] In fact, a number of men were cut down, but the battalion continued to advance. Lewis would recall *The Iliad* when he sought to describe the experience of coming under fire: "This is war. This is what Homer wrote about."[60] By 7:15 p.m., the assault was successful. Lewis safely reached the village, now in British hands, and received about sixty German prisoners.

A MAN OF CONSCIENCE

Nevertheless there were casualties, including Second Lieutenant Laurence Johnson, struck by machine-gun fire and dead the next day. He was twenty years old. Johnson had joined the army at about the same time as Lewis. The two met during military training at Oxford and found they had much in common. Both planned to take up their scholarship, their love of the classics, after the war. Both enjoyed debating the big questions about God, philosophy, and morality. Thrust into combat together, they found time to talk during lulls in the fighting.

"I had hoped to meet him at Oxford some day, and renew the endless talks that we had out there," Lewis wrote soon after learning of his death. "I had him so often in my thoughts. . . . I can hardly believe he is dead."[61] Reflecting years later, Lewis declared that Johnson "would have been a lifelong friend if he had not been killed." He even viewed Johnson's arrival in his battalion as a providential challenge to his atheism—"in my own battalion also I was assailed"—and a vital part of his eventual conversion to Christianity.[62] "In him I found dialectical sharpness such as I had hitherto known only in Kirk [Kirkpatrick], but coupled with youth and whim and poetry. He was moving toward Theism and we had endless arguments on that and every other topic whenever we were out of the line."[63]

Yet there was much more to Johnson that so deeply impressed Lewis beyond his debating skills: a quality of character that he had rarely encountered among his academic peers. Johnson possessed an unimpeachable integrity—a coherent moral code—that caught Lewis completely off guard: "The important thing was that he was a man of conscience. I had hardly till now encountered principles in anyone so nearly my own age and my own sort. The alarming thing was that he took them for granted. It crossed my mind for the first time since my apostasy that the severer virtues might have some relevance to one's own life."[64]

We cannot know exactly how Johnson's commitment to these "severer virtues" influenced Lewis in his journey toward Christian faith. But we know that he found it compelling—"I accepted his principles at once"—and that he was somewhat embarrassed by his own "unexamined life." Lewis would have to reckon with Johnson's principles, with the severity of the moral universe envisioned in the Bible, before his conversion could occur.[65]

Meanwhile, the assault at Riez du Vinage was still in play. The next morning, on April 15, the Germans counterattacked by bombing the village. The British returned fire. A shell—probably fired from behind the British line—went off close to Lewis, killing Sergeant Harry Ayres. His death was a great loss to Lewis: the sergeant had treated him with unusual respect and compassion and "became to me almost like a father."[66]

Shrapnel from the same mortar struck Lewis in the hand, leg, and chest. A stretcher crew picked him up and took him to No. 6 British Red Cross Hospital, near Étaples. His brother, also deployed in France, borrowed a motorbike and rushed over to see him.

With no life-threatening injuries, Lewis was sent home to England to make a full recovery. "Thank God Jacks has come through it safely," Warnie wrote in his journal, "and that nightmare is now lifted from my mind."[67] Lewis learned that the fragment in his chest was too close to his heart to be removed; it would have to stay. "They will leave it there," he wrote, "and I am told that I can carry it about for the rest of my life without any evil results."[68] Lewis would not rejoin his battalion before the war ended; his soldiering days were done.

"My life is rapidly becoming divided into two periods," he wrote, "one including all the time before we got into the battle of Arras, the other since."[69] From a hospital bed in Bristol, Lewis now struggled to come to terms with the face of war: the shattered limbs and shattered minds, the men who never returned, the randomness of death. In addition to Moore and Johnson, most of the remainder of his friends would die in battle in the last year of the war: Alexander Gordon Sutton, killed January 2; Thomas Kerrison Davy, who died of his wounds on March 29; and Martin Ashworth Somerville, killed in Palestine on September 21. "I could sit down and cry over the whole business: and yet of course we have both much to be thankful for," he wrote his father. "If I had not been wounded when I was, I should have gone through a terrible time. Nearly all my friends in the Battalion are gone."[70]

A GLIMPSE OF NARNIA

What Lewis and Tolkien and the fighting men of their generation endured was something novel in the history of warfare: modern science and technology ruthlessly devoted to the annihilation of both man and nature. Only a handful of statesmen openly worried about the infatuation with material and scientific advancement. Winston Churchill was one of them. "Without an equal growth of Mercy, Pity, Peace, and Love, Science herself may destroy all that makes life majestic and tolerable," he wrote. "There never was a time when the inherent virtue of human beings required more strong and confident expression in daily life."[71]

Lewis and Tolkien would use their literary gifts to contribute mightily to this task: the "confident expression" of human dignity in cultural life. At the same time, the abuse of science—its capacity to dehumanize its masters as well as its victims—would also be a major theme of their works. Rather than liberating human beings from their ancient frailties, science enslaved them. The dystopian world in Lewis's *That Hideous Strength*, for example, is dominated by an ostensibly scientific institute, the N.I.C.E., a cover for supernatural and sinister purposes. "There was now at last a real chance for fallen Man to shake off that limitation of his powers which mercy had imposed upon him as a protection from the full results of his fall," Lewis wrote. "If this succeeded, Hell would be at last incarnate."[72]

Like Tolkien, the experience of war cut in two directions for Lewis. He could never quite forget its depredations: "the frights, the cold, the smell of H.E. [high explosive], the horribly smashed men still moving like half-crushed beetles, the sitting or standing corpses, the landscape of sheer earth without a blade of grass, the boots worn day and night till they seemed to grow to your feet . . ."[73] And yet, as we'll see, the sorrows of war did not ultimately blacken Lewis's creative life. The world of Narnia, a land watered by streams of joy—"the land I have been looking for all my life"—would emerge from the wreckage of a Great War.

Perhaps something like Narnia became visible during a journey to a hospital in London, where Lewis was sent to recover from his wounds. It seems likely that the simple pleasure of a train ride through the English countryside, set against the dreariness and horror of war, created for Lewis a powerful experience of joy: a sensation so compelling that it undermined his materialist outlook. As he wrote from his bed at Endsleigh Palace Hospital:

> Can you imagine how I enjoyed my journey to London? First of all the sight and smell of the sea, that I have missed for so many long and weary months, and then the beautiful green country seen from the train. . . . I think I never enjoyed anything so much as that scenery—all the white in the hedges, and the fields so full of buttercups that in the distance they seemed to be of solid gold.[74]

The experience appears to have wrought a change in Lewis—a small change, perhaps, but a permanent one. It quickened his belief in a spiritual, otherworldly source of natural beauty. "You see the conviction is gaining ground on me that after all Spirit does exist," he wrote. "I fancy that there is Something right outside time & place, which did not create matter, as the Christians say, but is matter's great enemy: and that Beauty is the call of the spirit in that something to the spirit in us. You see how frankly I admit that my views have changed."[75]

Something "outside time and place" had stirred him. Perhaps the stirring began with George MacDonald and *Phantastes*, the book Lewis discovered during the war. This story of the human longing for beauty in the midst of sorrow and death would, in some respects, anticipate Lewis's own quest. "She smiled when she saw that my eyes were open," wrote MacDonald. "I asked her whether it was day yet. She answered, 'It is always day here, so long as I keep my fire burning.' I felt wonderfully refreshed; and a great desire to see more of the island awoke within me."[76]

CHAPTER 5

THE LAND OF
SHADOW

Three weeks after the German surrender at Compiegne on November 11, 1918, ending the First World War, the American president left for Europe to help broker the peace. In January, Woodrow Wilson had outlined his dream for a new global order, in his Fourteen Points, a document imbued with progressive assumptions about democracy, humanity, and international politics. Wilson's League of Nations would prevent another war, either through moral suasion or collective security. "They are the principles of mankind," he told the US Congress, "and they must prevail."

They would not prevail, of course, but many in Europe were not yet prepared to believe it. They wanted to believe that, under Wilson's enlightened leadership, democratic principles would govern the nations of the earth. All over Europe there were parks, squares, streets, and railway stations bearing Wilson's name. Posters declared, "We Want a Wilson Peace." Italians knelt in front of his image. In France, the left-wing newspaper *L'Humanite* devoted an issue to praising the American president. Nationalist movements from Korea to Arabia clung to the Fourteen Points as their lodestar.[1]

Thus, when Wilson arrived in Paris on December 13, throngs of admirers were there to greet him. They filled the streets, hung from windows, cheered from rooftops. "He was transfigured in the eyes of men," wrote H. G. Wells. "He ceased to be a common statesman; he became a Messiah." In a war that had devastated so many lives and nations, Europeans longed for a redemptive outcome. Wilson, as the leader of the only democracy that seemed capable of negotiating a just peace, held out the prospect of redemption. "Wilson kept alive the hope that human society, despite the evidence, was getting better, that nations would one day live in harmony," writes historian Margaret MacMillan. "In 1919, before disillusionment had set in, the world was more than ready to listen to him."[2]

Listening is one thing, however. Wilson believed that, armed only with rhetoric and idealism, he could remake international politics conform to his progressive, humanitarian vision. It was an impossible hope. The old rivalries and prejudices and power politics would reappear. The Treaty of Versailles, signed on June 28, 1919, proved a profound disappointment to just about everyone involved. The Germans felt betrayed by their leaders, while the victors lacked the will to enforce the treaty's provisions. "Is this the end?" asked Winston Churchill in *The World Crisis*. "Is it merely a chapter in a cruel and senseless story?"[3]

THE END OF ILLUSIONS

In the years after the conflict, the cruelty and senselessness of the war—of any war for any reason—became the dominant motifs of a generation. The writings of authors such as Robert Graves (*Goodbye to All That*), Siegfried Sassoon (*Memoirs of an Infantry Officer*), Ernest Hemingway (*A Farewell to Arms*), T. S. Eliot (*The Hollow Men*), and Erich Remarque (*All Quiet on the Western Front*) reinforced these themes in the public mind. The watchword was *disillusionment*: a new cynicism about liberal democracy, capitalism, Christianity, and the achievements of Western civilization.

Barbara Tuchman, in her Pulitzer Prize–winning book, *The Guns of August*, captured the postwar intellectual mood of millions:

> Men could not sustain a war of such magnitude and pain without hope—the hope that its very enormity would ensure that it could never happen again and the hope that when somehow it had been fought through to a resolution, the foundations of a better-ordered world would have been laid. . . . Nothing less could give dignity or sense to the monstrous offensives in which thousands and hundreds of thousands were killed to gain ten yards and exchange one wet-bottomed trench for another. When every autumn people said it could not last through the winter, and when every spring there was still no end in sight, only the hope that out of it all some good would accrue to mankind kept men and nations fighting. When at last it was over, the war had many diverse results, and one dominant one transcending all others: disillusion.[4]

Given the scale of human slaughter, how could it be otherwise?[5] The destructiveness of the First World War exceeded that of all other wars known in human history: more than sixteen million dead, twenty-one million wounded, hundreds of thousands buried in unmarked graves.

Most of the nations of Europe suffered grievous losses. Russia gave up 1.7 million men, another 5 million wounded. In Germany, roughly 465,000 soldiers were killed each year for the duration of the war. The generation of German men from nineteen to twenty-two years of age was reduced by 35 percent. In France, the casualty rate (dead or wounded) was an astonishing 75 percent. About 2 million French soldiers died, or roughly 25 percent of all the men in France, leaving behind 630,000 war widows. In Britain, 921,000 soldiers were dead, more than 2 million wounded; one of every three British households had a man killed, injured, or taken prisoner. The United States, which suffered the fewest casualties among the great powers, lost more than 116,000 men, and twice that number wounded.

Many civilians suffered and died during the war. The Allied blockade of Germany caused roughly 750,000 deaths from starvation and disease. In Serbia, with a prewar population of 5 million, about 125,000 were killed in action. But another 650,000 civilians died from disease or hunger—a total of 15 percent of the population lost. Massacres of civilians were carried out on a shocking scale, most notoriously by the Ottoman Turks against the Armenian minority: men, women, and children by the hundreds of thousands were executed, their bodies dumped in mass graves. "Those who were not killed at once were driven through mountains and deserts without food, drink, or shelter," writes historian David Fromkin. "Turkish Armenia was destroyed, and about half its people perished."[6] It was the first true genocide of the twentieth century.[7]

Europeans immediately embarked on a collective program of remembrance. Cemeteries and memorials devoted to the fallen began appearing all over the Continent. At large sites honoring the soldiers who fought at Verdun, Ypres, the Somme, and Meuse Argonne, the crosses and headstones seem to stretch into eternity. In Belgium, at Tyne Cot, the largest British war cemetery in the world, there are nearly twelve thousand graves. Between 1920 and 1923, Britain delivered four thousand headstones a week to France.[8] Indeed, Britain's sacrifice is recalled in virtually every cathedral in France, where a cross and tablet bear this inscription: "To the Glory of God and in memory of one million men of the British Empire who died in the Great War and of whom the greatest number rest in France." Throughout the 1920s and 1930s, hardly a year passed without a ceremony unveiling another imposing monument.[9]

Beginning in 1919, by the king's proclamation, Great Britain observed two minutes of silence at 11:00 a.m. on November 11, a tradition that continues to this day. In towns where Christian holidays such as Good Friday might be lightly observed, "it is Armistice Day that draws everyone to church."[10]

THE VERTIGO YEARS

The unprecedented butchery of the war produced not only a deep sense of grief and disillusionment. It created a feeling of helplessness, a psychological gloom among the survivors. It is an outlook expressed poignantly in the final pages of Remarque's memoir. *All Quiet on the Western Front* describes a generation of soldiers who will return to civilian life "weary, broken, burnt out, rootless, and without hope."[11] The mood was acute among writers, artists, and public intellectuals, but affected ordinary middle-class Europeans as well. "Dismay was a mainstream concern," writes historian Richard Overy in *The Twilight Years*. "For the generation living after the end of the First World War the prospect of imminent crisis, a new Dark Age, became a habitual way of looking at the world."[12]

Book titles tell much of the story: Spengler's *The Decline of the West* (1918); McCabe's *The End of the World* (1920); Freeman's *Social Decay and Degeneration* (1921); Webb's *The Decay of Capitalist Civilization* (1923); Muret's *The Twilight of the White Races* (1926); Kenworthy's *Will Civilization Crash?* (1927); Bond's *Racial Decay* (1928); Gibbs's *The Day After Tomorrow: What Is Going to Happen to the World?* (1928); Riddell's *Sterilization of the Unfit* (1929); Burns's *Modern Civilization on Trial* (1931); Milner's *The Problem of Decadence* (1931); Auden's *The Dance of Death* (1933); and Dearmer's *Christianity and the Crisis* (1933).

The fear that civilization was under threat was more than a literary trope. The concepts of decline and collapse, of sickness and death, infected nearly every cultural endeavor: intellectual, artistic, literary, scientific, philosophical, and religious.[13] For these thinkers, the notion of humanity's moral and spiritual progress lay in the dustbin of history. "We cannot help it if we are born as men of the early winter of full Civilization," wrote Spengler, "instead of on the golden summit of a ripe Culture."[14]

Although his Catholic faith remained intact, J. R. R. Tolkien later confessed that he "bemoaned the collapse of all my world" that began with his deployment to the Western Front.[15] Here he seemed to have in mind the frustration of his creative and intellectual longings; the war forced him to mostly put aside his imaginative powers just to survive. "It isn't the tough stuff one minds so much," he wrote later. "I was pitched into it all, just when I was full of stuff to write, and of things to learn; and never picked it all up again."[16]

Tolkien was demobilized from the British Expeditionary Force on July 16, 1919, and moved back to Oxford with his wife, Edith, and infant son, John. He joined the staff of the *New English Dictionary*, a cohort of experts at work on an exhaustive dictionary of the English language. Thrust into the role of the philologist, Tolkien excelled. His intellectual energies—his passion for the Anglo-Saxon and Germanic languages—had found a worthy outlet. As the dictionary's editor, Henry Bradley, described him at the time: "I have no hesitation in saying that I have never known a man of his age who was in these respects his equal."[17]

After serving as a professor of English Language at Leeds University, Tolkien won a professorship of Anglo-Saxon at Oxford in 1925. Nevertheless, his early academic success could not erase the heartache of war. Oxford University lost nearly one in five servicemen in the conflict. From Exeter College, Tolkien's college, 141 men had perished. Thus he experienced "a time of sorrow and mental suffering."[18] The loss of so many friends to the war produced, in the words of his children, "a lifelong sadness."[19]

When C. S. Lewis was demobilized from the army on Christmas Eve, 1918, he could hardly believe that the many months of anxiety—of having to return to the battle—had come to an end. "It is almost incredible that the war is over, isn't it," he wrote Arthur Greeves, "not to have the 'going back' hanging over my head all the time. This time last year I was in the trenches."[20] Lewis immediately left for Belfast to see his father and brother.

"It was as if the evil dream of four years had passed away and we were still in the year 1915," Warnie wrote in his diary. "In the evening there was bubbly for dinner in honor of the event."[21]

In January 1919, Lewis returned to Oxford, as did more than eighteen hundred ex-servicemen, to resume his studies in the classics at University College. The place was already abuzz with lectures and debates, making Lewis aware of "a great difference between this Oxford and the ghost I knew before." When the minutes from a 1914 meeting of one of Lewis's college clubs were read aloud, though, he was taken aback. "I don't know any little thing that has made me realize the absolute suspension and waste of these years more thoroughly."[22]

He mourned the passing of old friends. Upon hearing the news of the death of his mentor, William Kirkpatrick, Lewis confessed an internal struggle. "He is so indelibly stamped on one's mind once known, so often present in thought, that he makes his own acceptance of annihilation the more unthinkable," he wrote his father in 1921. "I have seen death fairly often and never yet been able to find it anything but extraordinary and rather incredible. The real person is so very real, so obviously living and different from what is left that one cannot believe something has turned into nothing."[23]

Though sensitive to religious questions, Lewis remained uncommitted. Still a young man, he already had experienced deep sorrow and struggle, and it left him with a sober, if not gloomy, view of the world. "The early loss of my mother, great unhappiness at school, and the shadow of the last war . . . had given me a pessimistic view of existence," he wrote years later. "My atheism was based on it."[24] He turned his heart and mind to literature; academic study absorbed him. "He has read more classics than any boy I ever had," Kirkpatrick once said of him. "He is a student who has no interest except in reading and study."[25] As Lewis expressed his outlook at the time, apart from the people who were important to him, "work is the only thing . . . that is worth caring about."[26]

In the winter of 1922, Lewis recorded in his diary a conversation with Dr. John Askins, the brother of Mrs. Moore, known as "the Doc." Askins had served as a captain in the Royal Army Medical Corps and was wounded in January 1917. He had come to stay with his sister for a few weeks, and one evening after dinner Lewis and Askins went for a walk. "We went beyond his lodgings to the end of Iffley village to look at the church and the trees in the starlight," he wrote. "I don't know how, but we fell to talking of death—on the material side—and all the other horrors hanging over one. The Doc said that if you stopped to think, you couldn't endure this world for an hour. I left him and walked home."[27]

Many postwar thinkers and writers, in fact, were unwilling to endure the world in its new form: a kind of spiritual vertigo took hold, a frantic search for solutions to the human predicament. Freudian psychology, eugenics, socialism, spiritualism, scientism—these and other ideologies were attempts to solve, or explain away, the horrors that seemed to be hanging over the human race. Though these ideas may have originated before the war, by the 1920s they were gaining ground rapidly in Europe and the United States.

UNLEASHING NEW PLAGUES

Indeed, it can be argued that the Great War launched three of the deadliest forces in the history of the West.

The first was Spanish influenza, which originated at a US Army base in Kansas in March 1918. The virus crossed Europe on crowded American troopships and spread throughout the Continent. Before it ran its course, upward of sixty million people—four times the number killed in the war—died from influenza worldwide. "The morticians worked day and night," recalled Josie Mabel Brown, a US Naval Nurse. "You could never turn around without seeing a big red truck being loaded with caskets for the train station so the bodies could be sent home."[28] In the midst of the outbreak, George Newman, Chief Medical Officer of Britain's Ministry of Health, proclaimed that influenza had "destroyed more human lives in a few months than did the European war in five years."[29]

Like the conflict that helped to launch the epidemic, the influenza of 1918 disproportionately killed young adults: men and women from fifteen to forty years of age, in the prime of their lives.[30] Victims displayed "the dreaded blueness" of the face, the sign of pneumonia, of the patient drowning in the fluids building up in the lungs. "This was an illness without precedent," writes historian Susan Kingsley Kent, "whose etiology and treatment could not be discerned or determined."[31] My grandmother, Esther Aiello, who lived in Brooklyn, New York, at the time, would recall those days with a sense of dread. "We used to watch them carry the bodies out of the houses," she said. "Everyone was afraid."[32]

The second epidemic was atheistic communism. When Russia pulled out of the war in early 1917, the days of the Tsarist regime were numbered. After the Romanov dynasty—which had ruled Russia for three centuries—finally collapsed, the emergence of a "Provisional Government" stirred hopes of a democratic revolution. "Good Lord, it's so great that Tsar Nicholas and the autocracy no longer exist!" wrote a Russian soldier in his diary. "This is the dawn of a great new Russia, happy and joyful. We soldiers are free men, we are equal, we are all citizens of Great Russia now!"[33]

Instead, the Bolsheviks, led by Leon Trotsky and Vladimir Lenin, strangled the nascent republican government in its crib. Enemies of the communist revolution—real and imaginary— were purged without conscience. Announced Trotsky: "We shall not enter into the kingdom of socialism in white gloves on a polished floor."[34] Thus a revolution waged in the name of bread, peace, and the proletariat produced a murderous civil war, mass starvation, and political dictatorship. By 1919, Lenin's policy of War Communism assimilated five million men into the Red Army, assuring the complete dominance of the Communist Party's Central Committee for decades to come. A profoundly materialistic, atheistic vision established itself in Russia—and with global ambitions.

The Great War seemed to confirm the fatal weakness of democratic capitalism, creating a susceptibility to all kinds of utopian schemes. When the Communist International held its first World Congress in 1919, it drew delegates from twenty-six European countries, as well as the United States. Socialism and communism found eager recruits in Great Britain. Lewis encountered quite a number of them at Oxford, and was disdainful: "I think we have now arrived at the point where a wise man can do no more than wait for the end with what grace he can," he wrote in August 1920. "And it is hard to summon much grace if you meet as many traitors and cranks in our own class as I do here, hankering for the blessing of Soviet rule at once."[35]

The third epidemic was fascism. It began in Italy in the 1920s, in a society that seemed to be in tatters. The war left the country with a startling degree of poverty and one of the highest inflation rates in Europe. The Italians were politically divided and disappointed; the parliamentary government was hopelessly corrupt, the monarchy unpopular. Many soldiers who returned to life as factory workers or clerks or shopkeepers found civilian life empty and uninspiring.

Enter Benito Mussolini. On October 28, 1922, with forty thousand "Blackshirts" under his command, Mussolini marched on Rome. King Victor Emmanuel and his embattled government lost heart. "Il Duce" became the first European leader to dispense with multi-party democracy. "The century of democracy is over," he proclaimed. "Democratic ideologies have been liquidated."[36] Mussolini was also the first to proclaim a new *fascist* regime, a word adopted from the Roman *fasces*, rods of punishment symbolizing the power of the state. As he wrote in his manifesto: "For the Fascist, everything is in the State, and nothing human or spiritual exists, much less has value, outside the State."[37]

An avid reader of modern thought, Mussolini, for all practical purposes, was an atheist. His first publication was a book called *God Does Not Exist*. His anti-clericalism, however, would not prevent him from manipulating the church for political purposes. "The influenza virus of 1918 had enveloped the world in weeks and penetrated almost everywhere," writes historian Paul Johnson. "The virus of force, terror and totalitarianism might prove equally swift and ubiquitous."[38] It did: by the mid-1920s, fascist groups appeared all over Europe, often supported by church leaders. In each case, they brought with them Mussolini's taste for political violence. Within a decade, fascist or quasi-fascist regimes would emerge in Spain, Portugal, Poland, Hungary, Austria, Greece, Romania—and Germany.

THE CRISIS OF FAITH

Thus the crisis of faith in postwar Europe was multilayered. There was an erosion of what might be called *civilizational confidence*, a widespread disillusionment with the West and its supposed cultural achievements. Liberal democracy, constitutionalism, capitalism, progressivism—all seemed in a state of near collapse. Wrote Gilbert Murray in *The Ordeal of This Generation* (1929): "The system which before the war was considered to be essential to civilization, at any rate if civilization was to advance, is now in peril of its life."[39] Since Christianity was considered integral to Europe's political and economic system, the perceived failure of that system was a spiritual failure as well.

The disintegration of orthodox Christian belief among all classes of Europeans during the 1920s, though easy to overstate, was real enough. "A profound sense of spiritual crisis was the hallmark of that decade," writes historian Modris Eksteins. "It affected rural laborers, large landowners, industrialists, factory workers, shop clerks and urban intellectuals."[40] There were numerous causes for the weakening of religious faith, but among the most important was the influence of Freudian psychology, which got an immense boost in the postwar years.

The experience of trench warfare produced many cases of mental disorders among soldiers and war veterans. It became known as *shell shock*: Well-bred men from upper-class or military families, who fought with distinction, who were decorated for valor, suddenly broke. They were neither cowardly nor insane.[41]

Mrs. Moore's brother, "the Doc," became stricken with the disorder, brought on by his combat experience. During one of his visits, he suffered repeated outbursts of extreme mental torture—he apparently believed he was going to hell—and was sent off to a hospital. Lewis spent many hours with him, trying to comfort him. "Nothing can wring the ghost of a smile from him," Lewis wrote in his diary. "For painfulness I think this beats anything I've seen in my life."[42] The Doc soon died from heart failure. "Isn't it a damned world," Lewis wrote to a friend, "and we thought we could be happy with books and music!"[43]

Freud seemed to offer an honorable explanation for the condition. His methods of psychoanalysis appeared preferable to the brutal alternatives available for curing mental illness: medication, verbal bullying, or electric-shock therapy. "When the electric current was increased," writes Paul Johnson, "men died under treatment, or committed suicide rather than face more, like victims of the Inquisition."[44]

When Freud's first psychiatric clinic opened in Berlin in 1920, it paved the way for his views about human nature, guilt, and God. Freud proved especially attractive to a generation struggling to find meaning in the war's aftermath. Religious belief was seen as an attempt to protect against suffering, "a delusional remolding of reality."[45] With God discredited, meaning must be found "in life itself, in the act of living, in the vitality of the moment."[46] Thus, the new psychology legitimized a new hedonism. Within a decade, W. R. Matthews, the Dean of Exeter, complained of "the decay of institutional religion" because of the "incoherence of the Christian message and its apparent contradiction with modern knowledge."[47]

All of this helped to produce the modern, secular zealot: the revolutionary who seeks to create heaven on earth. Science, psychology, politics, economics, education—any of these disciplines might be enlisted in the cause. At universities such as Oxford, where Tolkien and Lewis established themselves in the 1920s, a cocktail of experimentation and existential doubt was the order of the day.

Pacifism was all the rage. Patriotism was out, replaced by contempt for all the old virtues. For the intellectual class as well as the ordinary man on the street, the Great War had defamed the values of the Old World, along with the religious doctrines that helped to underwrite them. Moral advancement, even the idea of morality itself, seemed an illusion.

What Hemingway wrote in *A Farewell to Arms* captured the attitude of many soldiers and civilians alike. When laid beside the actual names of men and regiments that perished in the conflict, "abstract words such as glory, honor, courage, or hallow were obscene."[48] As Lewis recalled the scene many years later, the "mental climate of the Twenties" influenced an entire generation of students and future scholars. "None can give to another what he does not possess himself," he wrote. "A man whose mind was formed in a period of cynicism and disillusion, cannot teach hope or fortitude."[49] The verdict was in: the war to make the world safe for democracy, the holy war to advance Christian ideals, was an unholy delusion.

Given these postwar sensibilities, how did Oxford become the incubator for epic literature extolling valor and sacrifice in war?[50] Why would the works of Tolkien and Lewis, rooted in a narrative of Christian redemption, ever see the light of day?

TOLKIEN THE MYTHMAKER

The first story that Tolkien ever wrote down can be traced to his days as a soldier. In early 1917, when he was recovering at Great

Haywood from trench fever, he wrote "The Fall of Gondolin" and set the stage for his mythology about an epic struggle for Middle-earth. Writing mostly from his hospital bed, Tolkien produced a series of stories (later published as *The Book of Lost Tales*), which would inform his major works: *The Silmarillion*, *The Hobbit*, and *The Lord of the Rings*. Each involves a violent contest between good and evil—and in each there are hints of the horrors of the Somme.

In "The Fall of Gondolin" we read of the assault by Morgoth, the prime power of evil, against the last elvish stronghold. Although the city is "beleaguered without hope," there are "deeds of desperate valor" performed by the leaders of the noble houses and their warriors.[51] The tale bears the memories of the combat veteran:

> The fume of the burning, and the steam of the fair fountains of Gondolin withering in the flame of the dragons of the north, fell upon the vale of Tumladen in mournful mists; and thus was the escape of Tuor and his company aided. . . . Nonetheless they came thither, and beyond hope they climbed, in woe and misery, for the high places were cold and terrible, and they had among them many that were wounded, and women and children.[52]

Biographer Humphrey Carpenter sees in Tolkien's work an unexpected response to the First World War. He suggests that the central part of the story borrows from Tolkien's experiences on the Somme—"or rather to his reaction to those experiences, for the fighting at Gondolin has a heroic grandeur entirely lacking in modern warfare."[53] Years later, Tolkien admitted to his son, Christopher, then a soldier in the Second World War, that his earliest writings were a way of coping with the violence and suffering and anxieties of war. "I sense amongst all your pains (some merely physical) the desire to express your *feeling* about good, evil, fair, foul in some way: to rationalize it, and prevent it from festering," he wrote. "In my case it generated Morgoth and the History of the Gnomes."[54] Morgoth became the equivalent of Satan in Middle-earth, while the gnomes were reinvented as the race of elves who stand against him.

It seems that Tolkien, even in the throes of combat, consciously sought to retrieve a martial tradition that would become a casualty alongside all the other casualties of the First World War. Already he was constructing a mythology about England meant to recall its long history of struggle for noble purposes. "I was from early days grieved by the poverty of my own beloved country: it had no stories of its own (bound up with its tongue and soil), not of the quality that I sought," he once explained.[55] Thus he set out "to restore to the English an epic tradition and present them with a mythology of their own."[56]

Near the heart of this tradition are the concepts of honor and sacrifice for a just cause, themes that would of course animate *The Lord of the Rings*: "Now is the hour come, Riders of the Mark, sons of Eorl!" exclaims Théoden in *The Return of the King*. "Foes and fire are before you, and your homes far behind. Yet, though you fight upon an alien field, the glory that you reap there shall be your own for ever."[57] As an English soldier serving in France, Tolkien understood the difficulties of fighting "upon an alien field." He had his own doubts about the meaning of the war, and witnessed some of its fiercest scenes of slaughter. Yet he did not allow them to overwhelm his distinctively moral vision.

Many other authors, however, were moving in exactly the opposite direction.[58] Wilfred Owen, wounded three times before being killed in battle, wrote relentlessly in opposition to the war. His poems bear titles such as "Insensibility," "Mental Cases," "Futility," and "Disabled." In "Anthem for Doomed Youth," there is not a hint of nobility in the death of his fellow soldiers. "What passing-bells for these who die as cattle? / Only the monstrous anger of the guns."[59] Owen's friend, Siegfried Sassoon, who was awarded the Military Cross for bravery, nevertheless came to view the war as an immoral mistake. In the summer of 1917, Sassoon submitted a letter of protest to his commanding officer, calling the purposes of the war "evil and unjust." His poems are biting satires of the war and its effect on soldiers, with unsparing descriptions of "the land where all is ruin" and the "foundered trench-lines volleying doom for doom."[60]

Roughly four hundred "war novels" were published in the 1920s and 1930s, many of which helped to create a mythology of war as inherently ignoble and irrational.[61] One of the best-known works is *Goodbye to All That*, written by Robert Graves, who eagerly enlisted for officer training eight days after England declared war on Germany. Graves survived the Battle of the Somme, but sustained injuries that haunted him for the rest of his life. Less a memoir than a work of farce and theater, *Goodbye to All That* savages the absurdities and tragedies that seemed to characterize the war:

> The boast of every good battalion was that it·had never lost a trench; both our Line battalions made it—meaning that they had never been forced out of a trench without recapturing it before the action ended. Capturing a German trench

and being unable to hold it for lack of reinforcements did not count. . . . And, towards the end of the War, trenches could be honorably abandoned as being wholly obliterated by bombardment, or because not really trenches at all, but a line of selected shell-craters.[62]

Tolkien the ex-soldier could not glamorize combat. His letters to his sons during the Second World War, for example, are filled with great foreboding. "The utter stupid waste of war, not only material but moral and spiritual, is so staggering to those who have to endure it," he wrote. "But so short is human memory and so evanescent are its generations that in only about 30 years there will be few or no people with that direct experience which alone goes really to the heart. The burnt hand teaches most about fire."[63] Lewis was as familiar with the depredations of trench warfare as Tolkien, and one of the aspects of Tolkien's story that most impressed him was its realism:

This war has the very quality of the war my generation knew. It is all here: the endless, unintelligible movement, the sinister quiet of the front when "everything is now ready," the flying civilians, the lively, vivid friendships, the background of something like despair and the merry foreground, and such heaven-sent windfalls as a cache of choice tobacco "salvaged from a ruin."[64]

Nevertheless, Tolkien never intended to write a trench memoir. Instead, he set his mind to create a mythology worthy of his beloved England.[65] In addition to *The Book of Lost Tales*, he began work on *The Silmarillion*, where he explores the themes of evil, suffering, heroism, and death. An account of the First

Age, it tells the story of the fall of the most gifted among the Elves; their exile from Valinor (a kind of paradise); their return to Middle-earth, the place of their birth but now under the control of the Enemy; and their struggle against him, "the power of Evil still visibly incarnate."[66] It is here that Middle-earth first took on form and substance and became the battleground for the great conflict depicted in *The Lord of the Rings*.

Middle-earth is not, Tolkien insisted, an imaginary world, but rather *our* world—with its ancient truths and sorrows—set in a remote past. Indeed, any legends cast in the form of a supposed primitive history of this world, he said, must reckon with the tragic reality of human frailty.[67] As we'll see, Tolkien envisioned Middle-earth as the embodiment of a world struggling with the consequences of its Fall from Grace. "The theater of my tale is this earth, the one in which we now live. . . . The essentials of that abiding place are all there."[68]

LEWIS IN THE VALLEY OF DOUBT

C. S. Lewis might well have taken the path of other war authors and embraced the genre of irony and doubt. His earliest war writings suggest he was well on his way. Lewis's first published work, called "Death in Battle," appeared in *Reveille* magazine in 1919. The poem describes "the brutal, crowded faces around me, that in their toil have grown / into the faces of devils—yea, even as my own."[69] The work appeared in the same issue containing poems by Sassoon and Graves. In the same year Lewis published a collection of poems, written from 1915–1918, titled *Spirits in Bondage*. They embody an almost existential view of human life, ensnared in a cruel and unforgiving cosmos. In a letter to a friend,

Lewis explained the unifying theme: "that nature is wholly diabolical and malevolent and that God, if he exists, is outside of and in opposition to the cosmic arrangements."[70]

In "Ode for New Year's Eve," Lewis articulated the disenchantment, the sense that something has gone terribly wrong with all the supposed achievements of the West. The age of progress and innocence has vanished, he wrote, as if consumed wholesale in the furnace of the Great War:

> On upward curve and easily, for them both maid
> and man
> And beast and tree and spirit in the green earth
> could thrive.
> But now one age is ending, and God calls home
> the stars
> And looses the wheel of the ages and sends it
> spinning back
> Amid the death of nations, and points a
> downward track,
> And madness is come over us and great and
> little wars.[71]

Lewis's reference to "the death of nations" was not far off the mark. By the end of the First World War, entire empires had essentially collapsed—the Ottoman Empire, the Austro-Hungarian Empire, Tsarist Russia, and the German Empire—touching off revolutions and colonial rebellions around the world. In the process, a frightening share of young men were wiped out by death, emotionally debilitated by trench warfare, or permanently crippled. A small island nation, Britain nonetheless lost close to a

million of its citizens. "The effect of the war in Britain was catastrophic," writes Paul Fussell. "A whole generation was destroyed
that might have furnished the country's jurists, scholars, admin-
istrators, and political leaders."[72]

Neither can the "madness" of which Lewis wrote be denied.
The moral norms of European civilization seemed to perish
along with the human casualties. Although war always involves
great suffering, something had changed during the years of
1914–1918. "Europe and large parts of Asia and Africa became
one vast battlefield on which after years of struggle not armies
but nations broke and ran," observed Winston Churchill. "When
all was over, Torture and Cannibalism were the only two expedi-
ents that the civilized, scientific, Christian States had been able
to deny themselves: and these were of doubtful utility."[73]

The sheer destructive power of the war, the unimaginable
number of dead and wounded, the apocalyptic hopes and claims
of the participants, and the apparent futility of the outcome—
all of this instigated a new season of religious doubts and
experimentation.

Indeed, it is hard to overstate the spiritual crisis that overcame many young men and women, particularly among the
intellectuals, throughout the 1920s and 1930s. Swiss theologian
Karl Barth had been appalled at the wholehearted embrace of
Germany's war by the theologians, and at what he saw as the confusion of enlightened culture with the gospel. The Bible, Barth
insisted, contained "divine thoughts about men, not human
thoughts about God." Barth savaged the utopian schemes of
liberal Christianity in his monumental *Epistle to the Romans*
(1921). His work "burst like a bombshell on the playground of the
European theologians."[74]

Nevertheless, Barth's "neo-orthodoxy," as it came to be called, was being rejected by elite opinion throughout Europe and, increasingly, the United States. It came as a thunderbolt to the literati, for example, when T. S. Eliot was baptized and confirmed into the Church of England in 1927. How could the author of *The Wasteland* find solace in such a primitive superstition? How could a member of the literary set, London's Bloomsbury Group, commit such an act of intellectual betrayal?[75] Virginia Woolf expressed the indignation of her peers in a letter to a friend:

> I have had a most shameful and distressing interview with dear Tom Eliot, who may be called dead to us all from this day forward. He has become an Anglo-Catholic believer in God and immortality, and goes to church. I was shocked. A corpse would seem to me more credible than he is. I mean, there's something obscene in a living person sitting by the fire and believing in God.[76]

The obscenity of belief in God: such was the tide of elite opinion in much of postwar Europe. To many of the best and brightest, Christianity appeared to lack any explanatory power. It could neither account for the internecine conflict of the supposed Christian nations of Europe, nor offer a realistic hope of achieving a more peaceful and just global order. Rather, the church of the modern age seemed tethered to destructive doctrines and medieval superstitions.

"We find at the present day among the educated classes . . . a great output of new and more or less fantastic superstitions drawn indifferently from the mysterious East or the neurotic

West," wrote Gilbert Murray in *The Ordeal of This Generation* (1928). "Also a large and outspoken rejection of all religion and particularly of all morality."[77] Nietzsche had hailed this latter prospect at the end of the nineteenth century: "Perhaps the most solemn concepts which have occasioned the most strife and suffering, the concepts of 'God' and 'sin,' will one day seem to us of no more importance than a child's toy and a child's troubles seem to an old man."[78]

THE "GREAT WAR" WITH OWEN BARFIELD

Thus it is no surprise that postwar Oxford was becoming a hotbed of agnosticism, religious indifference, and experimentation. C. S. Lewis found himself entangled in an "unholy muddle" of competing philosophies, from psychoanalysis to rationalism. "And all the time . . . there's the danger of falling back into the most childish superstitions, or of running into dogmatic materialism to escape them."[79] As biographer George Sayer sums up the mood: "Most tutors encouraged their pupils above all to doubt."[80]

A lively specimen was Owen Barfield, a war veteran studying English literature whom Lewis met in 1919. Although Lewis agreed with Owen on almost nothing—"he has read all the right books but got the wrong thing out of every one"—a lifelong admiration and friendship began. Barfield became a devotee of "anthroposophy," a spiritual philosophy developed by Rudolf Steiner, which envisioned mankind as an integral part of the creative thought and evolution of the world. Lewis rejected Barfield's anthroposophy as a kind of Gnosticism, and the two initiated what they called a "Great War" of intellectual debate. It was another relationship that would alter the course of Lewis's intellectual and spiritual life:

> He is as fascinating (and infuriating) as a woman. When you set out to correct his heresies, you find he forsooth has decided to correct yours! And then you go at it, hammer and tongs, far into the night, night after night, or walking through fine country that neither gives a glance to, each learning the weight of the other's punches, and often more like mutually respectful enemies than friends. Actually (though it never seems so at the time) you modify one another's thought; out of this perpetual dogfight a community of mind and a deep affection emerge. But I think he changed me a good deal more than I him.[81]

In their "perpetual dogfight"—a phrase lifted from the war, of course—Barfield influenced Lewis in at least two profoundly important ways. He persuaded Lewis to abandon his "chronological snobbery," the assumption that the dominant intellectual fashion of the day makes every mode of thought from the past either suspect or irrelevant. This philosophical pose, given birth by the Enlightenment, grew to maturity after the conflagration of the First World War, into which so many cherished Victorian ideals had vanished.

Barfield also challenged the scientific and materialist view of reality typical among Oxford dons. The "old beliefs" central to Christianity were languishing after a radical assault from various quarters. Darwin, Nietzsche, Freud—in one form or another they and others mocked the notion of the sacred dignity of the individual. A great many educated Europeans and Americans had come to believe that the "aesthetic" experiences—our sense of morality, the longing for joy, and the love of beauty—were essentially meaningless. Though these intellectual movements could be hostile toward one another, Lewis realized they were united in their hatred of the "immortal longings" of ordinary human beings. "These people seemed to me to be condemning what they did not understand."[82]

Barfield's spiritualism, for all its eccentricities, appeared to offer a better explanation for these experiences than that of the materialist. He helped Lewis to consider the possibility that our moral intuitions, our aesthetic experiences, could lead us to objective truth: imagination might be as good a guide to reality as rational argument.

In a letter dated September 25, 1920, Lewis admitted to another Oxford friend that his studies in philosophy were leading him away from dogmatic skepticism. Addressed to Leo Baker, a pilot in the Royal Air Force during the war, the letter revealed a growing frustration with purely materialistic views of the universe. "I have no business to object to the universe as long as I have nothing to offer myself," he explained.

> You will be interested to hear that in the course of my philoso-phy—on the existence of matter—I have had to postulate some sort of God as the last objectionable theory: but of course we know nothing. At any rate we don't know what the real Good is, and consequently I have stopped defying heaven: it can't know less than I, so perhaps things really are alright. This, to you, will be old news, but perhaps you will see it in me as a sign of grace.[83]

By 1925 Lewis had cast off the stern atheism of his younger days. "It will be a comfort to me all my life to know that the scientist and the materialist have not the last word," he wrote, "that Darwin and Spencer, undermining ancestral beliefs, stand themselves on a foundation of sand."[84] Lewis's postwar friendships prevented him from adopting the moral indifference—what he called the "shallow pessimisms"—so typical of his generation.[85] They pressed upon him questions for which he had no credible answer. "Now that I have found, and am still finding more and more the element of truth in the old beliefs, I feel I cannot dismiss even their dreadful side so cavalierly," he wrote to Arthur Greeves. "There must be something in it: only what?"[86]

WHEN MYTH BECOMES FACT

This is the question that lies behind the famous late-night debate between C. S. Lewis and J. R. R. Tolkien in September 1931. It was a remarkable moment: a probing discussion of ancient myths and an ancient faith, it nonetheless speaks to the mystery of the modern predicament. Their exchange—an encounter between intensely creative minds over the meaning of Christianity—should be ranked as one of the most transformative conversations of the twentieth century.

Lewis was elected as a fellow and tutor in English Language and Literature at Oxford's Magdalen College in May 1925, the same year that Tolkien was elected a professor of Anglo-Saxon at Pembroke College. The two met for the first time a year later and realized that, despite their different approaches to literature, they had many shared interests and authors, including an attraction to mythologies. When Tolkien started a club among the dons to read Icelandic sagas, Lewis happily joined. It was called the Coalbiters—from the Icelandic *Kolbitar*—a term meaning "men who lounge so close to the fire in winter that they bite the coal."

During the next several years, as they met together, Lewis and Tolkien realized that they shared a love for "Northernness," the mythologies and fairy stories they had first encountered in the works of William Morris and George MacDonald and other authors.[87] In a letter to Arthur Greeves dated December 3, 1929, Lewis described one of their exchanges: "I was up till 2:30 on Monday, talking to the Anglo Saxon professor Tolkien, who came back with me to College from a society and sat discoursing of the gods and giants of Asgard for three hours, then departing in the wind and rain—who could turn him out, for the fire was bright and the talk good."

A deep friendship was taking root. And yet for all their mutual interests in literature, the two men could not agree on the nature of myth and its relationship to belief in God. The argument came to a head on Saturday evening, September 19, 1931.

Lewis had invited Tolkien and another friend, Hugo Dyson, to dine with him at Magdalen College. Dyson, a war veteran, had fought at the Battle of the Somme and was severely injured at the Battle of Passchendaele at Ypres. He was named a Lecturer in English at Reading University. Lewis liked him immensely at their first meeting, describing him as "a man who really loves truth: a philosopher and a religious man."[88] After the meal, Lewis took his friends to Addison's Walk, a tree-lined footpath that snakes along the River Cherwell near Magdalen College. As they walked they discussed and debated their ideas about metaphor and myth.[89]

To Lewis, myths might be beautiful, they might charm our imaginations, but they were lies: inventions that contain no objective truth about the world. This is what troubled Lewis about Christianity. It was like the Norse myth of the dying god Balder, a lovely fiction, "one mythology among many." Here was the "recognized scientific account" of the growth of religion that Lewis had written about to Arthur Greeves. It is the idea that "most legends have a kernel of fact in them somewhere," but enthusiasts transform the kernel into a glorified sun god, corn deity, or supernatural messiah. Lewis's critique represented the dominant academic view of religion by the turn of the century:

> When I say "Christ" of course I mean the mythological being into whom he was afterwards converted by popular imagination. . . . That the man Yeshua or Jesus did actually exist, is as certain as that the Buddha did actually exist: Tacitus mentions his execution in the Annals. But all the other tomfoolery about virgin birth, magic healings, apparitions and so forth is on exactly the same footing as any other mythology.[90]

Tolkien's view was exactly the opposite: myths did not originate with man, but with God. They are his means of communicating at least a portion of his truth to the world. Because men and women come from God, Tolkien argued, their highest ideals and longings come from him as well. It is not only man's abstract reasoning, but *also his imaginative inventions* that find their origin in God.[91] As such, they suggest an aspect of divine truth.

Mythmaking, what Tolkien calls "mythopoeia," is a way of fulfilling God's purposes as the Creator. By inventing a myth—by populating a world with elves and orcs, dragons and witches, gods and goddesses—the storyteller tries to retrieve the world he knew before man's fall from grace. "There was an Eden on this very unhappy earth," Tolkien explained many years later. "We all long for it, and we are constantly glimpsing it: our whole nature at its best and least corrupted, its gentlest and most humane, is still soaked with the sense of 'exile.' "[92] The mythmaker, fired by the sense of exile and the desire to return to his authentic home, reflects "a splintered fragment of the true light."[93]

Recounting their conversation in his poem "Mythopoeia," Tolkien insisted that pagan myths were not simply "lies," as Lewis claimed, but contained intimations of the truth about God and the world he has made, however disfigured:

> *The heart of man is not compound of lies,*
> *But draws some wisdom from the only Wise*
> *And still recalls him. Though now long estranged,*
> *Man is not wholly lost nor wholly changed.*
> *Dis-graced he may be, yet is not dethroned,*
> *And keeps the rags of lordship once he owned.*[94]

The friends finally returned to Lewis's study, where they talked until 3:00 a.m. The subject was Christianity. Lewis did not understand the meaning of the central teachings of the faith: the concepts known as "the blood of the Lamb" and "the atonement." How could the life and death of Jesus have "saved the world"? How could the sacrificial death of someone two thousand years ago help us now? It all seemed irrelevant and incomprehensible.[95]

Tolkien answered him immediately, and in his answer he revealed the core of his own philosophy as a writer and as a Christian thinker.[96] Yes, the story of Jesus the Christ is a kind of myth: it is the authentic story of the Dying God who returns to life to rescue his people from sin and death and bring them to "the Blessed Land," where "though they make anew, they make no lie."[97] The difference between Christianity and all the pagan myths is that this Dying God actually entered into history, lived a real life, and died a real death.

"Do you mean," Lewis asked, "that the story of Christ is simply a true myth, a myth that works on us in the same way as the others, but a myth that has *really happened*? In that case, I begin to understand."[98]

Years later, Lewis explained that his understanding of the nature of myth was crucial to his conversion. He finally concluded that paganism was "only a prophetic dream" and perhaps one of the "good dreams" that God sends to men and women to help guide them in their quest. Lewis's own quest would lead him back to the life of Jesus, to the Gospels, which he had begun to read regularly in their original Greek. "If ever a myth had become fact, had been incarnated, it would be just like this. And nothing else in all of literature was just like this," he wrote. "Here and here only in all time the myth must have become fact."[99]

Tolkien finally excused himself to return home, while Lewis and Dyson continued to talk until 4:00 a.m. An intellectual barrier to faith had collapsed. Twelve days later Lewis confessed to Arthur Greeves: "I have just passed on from believing in God to definitely believing in Christ—in Christianity. I will try to explain this another time. My long night talk with Dyson and Tolkien had a great deal to do with it."[100]

THE GREAT COLLABORATION

Lewis would devote much of the rest of his professional life to explaining Christianity to an uncomprehending world. In both his fiction and prose, in works such as *The Screwtape Letters*, *The Great Divorce*, and *Mere Christianity*, Lewis traced the movement of a human soul from doubt to belief. By his own account, there were many friendships and authors who played a part in his journey, his "Pilgrim's Regress."[101] His conversation with Tolkien, though, was the immediate human link in the chain. It left him with no rationalizations to fall back upon. "Everything that I had labored so hard to expel from my own life seemed to have flared up and met me in my best friends," he wrote. "Everyone and everything had joined the other side."[102]

Lewis's conversion was not only deep and vital, it was "the chief watershed in his life," writes biographer Walter Hooper. "There was no nook or cranny of his being that it did not eventually reach and transform."[103] His faith was nurtured by friendship: he and Tolkien formed the nucleus of a small group of writers— nearly all of them serious Christians—who met weekly in Lewis's rooms at Magdalen. They gathered to read aloud and critique each other's works. "Theoretically to talk about literature," Lewis explained, "but in fact nearly always to talk about something better."[104] They called themselves "the Inklings," those who "dabble in ink."[105]

It was in this setting that Lewis tested his first effort at science fiction as a vehicle for Christian truth. A pupil of his took seriously the dream of interplanetary colonization, which Lewis saw as a scientific attempt to defeat death—and as rival to Christianity. The result was *Out of the Silent Planet* (1938), the first of a science-fiction trilogy awash in religious themes and imagery. Lewis had read the novel aloud to the Inklings, where, according to Tolkien, it was "highly approved."[106] The book helped to launch Lewis's career as a popular writer. Yet without Tolkien's letter of praise to a publisher—much of it was dismissed as "bunk" by a reader assigned to the manuscript—the story might never have seen the light of day. "I read the story in the original manuscript and was so enthralled that I could do nothing else until I had finished it," Tolkien said. "I at any rate should have bought this story at almost any price if I had found it in print."[107]

Early reviews of the book were mostly positive, but Lewis was stunned to realize that almost no one discerned in it the biblical doctrine of the fall, which anchors the entire story. "If only there were someone with a richer talent and more leisure, I believe this great ignorance might be a help to the evangelization of England," he wrote to a friend. "Any amount of theology can now be smuggled into people's minds under cover of romance without their knowing it."[108] Here is an insight Lewis surely encountered in his many conversations with J. R. R. Tolkien.

At the same time, Lewis's influence on his friend would be profound. Tolkien had long believed that the "fairy-story" was really a genre for adults and "one for which a starving audience exists."[109] But that belief remained an untested proposition until Tolkien shared his early work with Lewis, who found it compelling. "If they won't write the kind of books we want to read," Lewis told his friend, "we shall have to write them ourselves."[110]

They made good on that pledge. Tolkien's *The Hobbit* is a story set "long ago in the quiet of the world, when there was less noise and more green."[111] Its chief character is Bilbo Baggins, a smallish creature known as a hobbit, an inhabitant of the bucolic Shire. He displays the virtues and vices of a middle-class Englishman. He has a comfortable life and shows no interest in adventures: "I can't think what anybody sees in them." Explained Tolkien: "The Hobbits are just rustic English people, made small in size because it reflects the generally small reach of their imagination—not the small reach of their courage or latent power."[112]

By the time *The Hobbit* was completed, Bilbo Baggins had endured a perilous quest through Middle-earth and joined an army of elves, men, and dwarves to face goblins and wild wolves in a final terrible battle. "Victory now vanished from hope. They had only stemmed the first onslaught of the black tide."[113]

Following the book's publication in 1937, Lewis praised it as "the *adaptation to children* of part of a huge private mythology of a most serious kind: the whole cosmic struggle as he sees it but mediated through an imaginary world."[114] This was precisely the task that Lewis himself took up in *The Chronicles of Narnia*, a series of stories for children about a hidden world caught up in a great contest between Good and Evil.

The instant popularity of Tolkien's fairy tale set him to work on "a new story about Hobbits." It is doubtful, though, that Tolkien would have finished his masterwork, *The Lord of the Rings*, without the enthusiasm and support of his friend. The two spent many hours in Lewis's rooms at Magdalen College, with Tolkien reading chapters out loud to a captive audience. "C. S. L. had a passion for hearing things read aloud, a power of memory for things received in that way," Tolkien explained, "and also a facility in extempore criticism."[115] Tolkien once recalled a lunch at which Lewis browbeat him to pick up the work again, which had stalled for quite some time. "The indefatigable man read me part of a new story!" Tolkien said. "But he is putting the screw on me to finish mine. I needed some pressure, and shall probably respond."[116] Tolkien's book dragged on for years, unfinished.

"I have drained the rich cup and satisfied a long thirst," Lewis wrote to Tolkien after reading the typescript of *The Lord of the Rings*. "No romance can repel the charge of 'escapism' with such confidence. If it errs, it errs in precisely the opposite direction: the sickness of hope deferred and the merciless piling up of odds against the heroes are near to being too painful."[117] Reflecting later on Lewis's long engagement with his story, Tolkien's gratitude is manifest. "The unpayable debt" he owed to Lewis, he said, was his "sheer encouragement"—over many years—to keep on. "He was for long my only audience," Tolkien explained. "Only from him did I ever get the idea that my 'stuff' could be more than a private hobby. But for his interest and unceasing eagerness for more I should never have brought The L. of the R. to a conclusion."[118]

Their collaboration, and the literary efforts which grew from it, could hardly come at a moment of greater crisis in the West. The generation of Tolkien and Lewis had passed through the most devastating conflict in history—with almost nothing to show for it. Nearly every noble belief and aspiration of their society seemed a falsehood, a fool's errand, a child's nursery tale. The Enlightenment project, with its idolization of reason, had run its course—straight into "that Ditch into which the blind hath led the blind in all ages, and have both there miserably perished."[119]

A world that once felt as solid and dependable as granite had become a land of shadows. Philip Gibbs, a journalist and novelist who served as one of Britain's official correspondents during the war, witnessed the collapse up close. "They had been taught to believe that the whole object of life was to reach out to beauty and love, and that mankind, in its progress to perfection, had killed the beast instinct, cruelty, blood-lust, the primitive, savage law of survival by tooth and claw and club and ax," he wrote. "All poetry, all art, all religion had preached this gospel and this promise. Now that ideal was broken like a china vase dashed to the ground."[120]

THE MORAL IMAGINATION

A counterfeit gospel, a false myth, created a cacophony of despair in the West. Yet two friends and authors refused to succumb to this storm of doubt and disillusionment. Fortified by their faith, they proclaimed for their generation—and ours—a True Myth about the dignity of human life and its relationship to God. Against all expectation, their writings would captivate and inspire countless readers from every culture and every part of the globe.

What explains their enduring influence? As mythmakers they create new worlds. They invent new languages. They transport us into realms of brooding darkness and unforgettable beauty. Yet their mythic imagination only partly accounts for their influence.

As we will see, it is their *moral imagination* that exerts a unique power: the proposition that every person is caught up in an epic contest between Light and Darkness. In the worlds of Tolkien and Lewis, the choices of the weak matter as much as those of the mighty. Here we are not left as orphans, for a force of Goodness stands ready to help. Here we meet Gandalf the Grey, the wisest and best of wizards, engaged in a titanic struggle against the Shadow that threatens Middle-earth; and Aslan, the fearsome Lion, who will pay any price to rescue Narnia from the "force of evil" that has entered it.

The great achievement of Tolkien and Lewis is the creation of mythic and heroic figures who nevertheless make a claim upon our concrete and ordinary lives. Through them we are challenged to examine our deepest desires, to shake off our doubts, and to join in the struggle against evil. For in their voice is a warning: a call to "do the deed at hand" no matter what the cost. In their presence is strength: the grace to "cast aside regret and fear," grace beyond all hope.[121] These are the great themes that dominate their works and continue to delight generations of readers.

In *The Lord of the Rings*, it is Gandalf who summons men to battle, whose presence demands a response of the heart. "'And now,' said the wizard, turning his back to Frodo, 'the decision lies with you. But I will always help you.' He laid his hand on Frodo's shoulder. 'I will help you bear this burden, as long as it is yours to bear. But we must do something, soon. The Enemy is moving.'"[122]

In *The Chronicles of Narnia*, it is Aslan whose voice must be reckoned with like no other, a voice that fills every soul with fear or delight. "Aslan threw up his shaggy head, opened his mouth, and uttered a long, single note; not very loud, but full of power. Polly's heart jumped in her body when she heard it. She felt sure that it was a call, and that anyone who heard that call would want to obey it and (what's more) would be able to obey it, however many worlds and ages lay between."[123]

CHAPTER 6

THAT HIDEOUS STRENGTH

I n the summer of 430 BC, the civilized world seems to be unraveling in the fog and fury of a great war.

It is the early phase of the Peloponnesian War, a vicious clash of imperial ambitions between the two titans of ancient Greece, Athens and Sparta. When the Athenian historian, Thucydides, set out to chronicle the war, he expected it would be "more momentous than any previous conflict." He was right. The war would envelop virtually the whole of the Greek world. It would drag on for twenty-seven years, anticipating the suffering and deprivation associated with modern conflicts: the atrocities, refugees, disease, starvation, and slaughter. It would destroy what was left of Athenian democracy.

In the second year of the conflict, a mysterious plague breaks out in Athens. It spreads rapidly, killing virtually everyone it touches, and sends the population into a state of panic and despair. "No particular constitution, strong or weak, proved sufficient in itself to resist," wrote Thucydides, "but the plague carried off all indiscriminately, and whatever the regime of care."[1] What follows is the complete breakdown in public and private morality: friends are left to die alone, family members flee their own households, mothers abandon their own children. Thucydides recorded the scene thus:

> No one was prepared to persevere in what had once been thought the path of honor, as they could well be dead before that destination was reached. Immediate pleasure, and any means profitable to that end, became the new honor and the new value. No fear of god or human law was any constraint. Pious or impious made no difference in their view, when they could see all dying without distinction.[2]

We have seen how despair and disbelief afflicted much of the generation that lived through the fires of the First World War. "It rose out of the peculiar conditions of trench warfare," writes G. J. Meyer, "an experience beyond anything the human psyche was built to endure."[3] Soldiers could not grasp what was happening to them. Tens of thousands were overwhelmed by shell shock. In Britain alone, four years after the end of the war, six thousand veterans were confined to insane asylums.[4] Postwar writers seemed to have no mental category for the nature of the conflict, no set of beliefs to understand it. This fact makes the literary aims of J. R. R. Tolkien and C. S. Lewis all the more remarkable: they steadfastly rejected the sense of futility and agnosticism that infected so much of the output of their era.

When the first book of Tolkien's trilogy, *The Fellowship of the Ring*, appeared in 1954, his Oxford friend wrote a review for *Time and Tide*. Lewis frankly acknowledged that Tolkien's story about hobbits and elves and wizards was a romantic, fantastical tale thoroughly out of step with the times. Here, like nowhere else, the heroic romance "has suddenly returned at a period almost pathological in its anti-romanticism."[5] Nevertheless, Lewis insisted, one of the surprising strengths of the story was its realism: the description of a titanic struggle between Good and Evil that navigates between the deadly reefs of illusion and disillusionment.

> As for escapism, what we chiefly escape is the illusions of our ordinary life. We certainly do not escape anguish. Despite many a snug fireside and many an hour of good cheer to gratify the Hobbit in each of us, anguish is, for me, almost the prevailing note. But not, as in the literature most typical of our age, the anguish of abnormal or contorted souls; rather that anguish of those who were happy before a certain darkness came up and will be happy if they live to see it gone.[6]

The same can be said of Lewis's stories as well. The most memorable scenes in *The Chronicles of Narnia* or *The Space Trilogy* typically bear this mark: the admixture of tragedy and hope. Like Tolkien, Lewis clothed his tales in fantasy and myth to convey hard truths about the human condition: its darkness and futility, as well as its virtues and triumphs. "And Man as a whole, Man pitted against the universe," he wrote, "have we seen him at all till we see that he is like a hero in a fairy tale?"[7] Presented as fantasies, these stories are intended to soften our modern prejudices and speak into our imagination. They thus allow us to rediscover truths about ourselves and our world that may otherwise lay hidden.

This helps to explain the extraordinary appeal of their works, which remain popular seventy years or more after first appearing in print. In a 2003 survey conducted by the BBC in Britain, *The Lord of the Rings* was found to be "the Nation's best-loved book." Tolkien has been praised as "the author of the century," and with good reason.[8] "In any study of modern heroism," writes Roger Sale, "if J. R. R. Tolkien's *The Lord of the Rings* did not exist, it would have to be invented."[9] Translated into thirty-eight languages, the trilogy has sold more than 150 million copies.

C. S. Lewis has earned comparable acclaim. *The Chronicles of Narnia* is widely considered a classic in children's fantasy, alongside the works of Lewis Carroll, Rudyard Kipling, and others. The series has sold more than 100 million copies and been translated into forty-seven languages. Even Philip Pullman's popular trilogy, *His Dark Materials*, a self-conscious repudiation of Lewis's work, pays homage to its narrative power. Movie adaptations of *The Lord of the Rings* and *The Chronicles of Narnia* have introduced hundreds of millions of people to their essentially Christian vision of the human story.

THE WORLD AS WE FIND IT

What are the basic elements of this vision? As soldiers in the Great War, Tolkien and Lewis endured a human cataclysm that laid a foundation for their mythic imagination. It thrust upon them as young men the experience of combat, suffering, and death that would remain with every war veteran of their generation.

"Your teeth are grinding on the fuse-pin of the hand-grenade.

The encounter will be short and murderous," wrote Ernst Jünger in *Storm of Steel*, one of the earliest memoirs of the First World War. "You tremble with two contradictory impulses: the heightened awareness of the huntsman, and the terror of the quarry. You are a world to yourself, saturated with the appalling aura of the savage landscape."[10] The German artist Otto Dix survived combat in Champagne, the Somme, and Russia, but it changed him. "Lice, rats, barbed wire, fleas, shells bombs, underground caves, corpses, blood, liquor, mice, cats, artillery, filth, bullets, mortars, fire, steel: that is what war is," he wrote. "It is the work of the devil."[11]

Tolkien and Lewis would essentially agree. Central to their experience was an encounter with the presence of evil: the deep corruption of the human heart that makes it capable of hunting down and destroying millions of lives in a remorseless war of attrition.[12]

A conviction emerged in both these authors, however, that the problem of evil was not explainable only in natural terms. Rather, evil existed as a darkness in the soul of every human being *and* as a tangible, spiritual force in the world. "The Shadow of that hideous strength," wrote Scottish poet Sir David Lyndsay, "six miles and more it is of length."[13] Like the war they knew on the Western Front, the Shadow is a dehumanizing force. It seeks to dominate or destroy anything that resists its will. This is the irrepressible fact behind their stories, the reality that flings their characters into action.

In *The Lord of the Rings*, Bilbo Baggins, owner of a mysterious Ring, returns home and is greeted by his close friend, the wizard Gandalf. Gandalf insists that Bilbo give the Ring to his young heir, Frodo Baggins. The Ruling Ring has special powers: its wearer, becoming invisible, could see the thoughts of all those who used the lesser rings, and could control and ultimately enslave them. Created by the Dark Lord Sauron, the Ring would become the ultimate weapon in his campaign to dominate all of Middle-earth. Sauron will do anything to retrieve it. As Gandalf explains:

> One Ring to rule them all, One Ring to find them,
> One Ring to bring them all, and in the darkness
>   bind them,
> In the land of Mordor where the shadows lie.

When Gandalf visits Frodo he warns of the impending danger and what must be done to overcome it. The Ring, he says, is a corrupting power. Anyone who continues to use it will be destroyed by it. There are no hands, no matter how pure, that can be trusted with the Ring for long: such is its force that it turns every good motive toward evil.

> A mortal, Frodo, who keeps one of the Great Rings, does not die, but he does not grow or obtain more life, he merely continues, until at last every minute is a weariness. And if he often uses the Ring to make himself invisible, he fades: he becomes in the end invisible permanently, and walks in the twilight under the eye of the Dark Power that rules the Rings . . . sooner or later, the Dark Power will devour him.[14]

Such a weapon, we learn, cannot be buried or hidden away. It must be destroyed. And the only place where it can be destroyed is the place where it was made: in the flames of Mount Doom in Mordor. "There lies our hope, if hope it be," says Elrond. "We must send the Ring to the Fire."[15] The Ring must be taken to Mordor. It is decided that Frodo will assume this awesome burden. This becomes his great quest—or, rather, his anti-quest, since his mission is not one of rescue, but of destruction.[16]

Frodo, as the Ring-bearer, senses a force of evil pressing in upon him as he and his companion, Sam Gamgee, approach the Gates of Mordor. It is the Eye of Sauron, "wreathed in flame," which searches relentlessly for the Ring in order to draw it home. "That horrible growing sense of a hostile will that strove with great power to pierce all shadows of cloud, and earth, and flesh, and to see you: to pin you under its deadly gaze, naked, and immovable," wrote Tolkien. "He was facing it, and its potency beat upon his brow."[17]

Lewis understood evil in much the same way: it is an objective power in the world, waging a war for individual souls. It seeks to create a society of slaves, ruled by despots, and "held together entirely by fear and greed."[18]

In *The Chronicles of Narnia*, Lewis set out in seven novels the unfolding history of the imaginary realm of Narnia—a realm torn apart by war. We trace the adventures of English children from the real world (modern-day London) who are magically transported into Narnia, a land of mythical beasts (fauns, satyrs, and centaurs) and talking animals (bears, badgers, moles, and mice). There they meet Aslan, the great Lion and "king of the Wood and son of the great Emperor-beyond-the-Sea." Aslan calls upon them to help rescue Narnia from a new despotism and to restore the throne of Narnia to its rightful line of kings.

No sooner do the four Pevensie children—Peter, Susan, Edmund, and Lucy—enter Narnia than they encounter a force of evil. It is the figure of Jadis, the Wicked Queen of Charn. She is a witch, and witches "are not interested in things or people unless they can use them."[19] Though she was once defeated, Jadis has been revived thanks to human folly. "The White Witch? Who is she?" asks Lucy. "Why, it is she who has got all Narnia under her thumb," says the Faun. "It's she who makes it always winter. Always winter and never Christmas; think of that!"[20]

In *The Magician's Nephew*, the children hear a sound emanating from the depths of the earth, a wondrous voice—"the First Voice"—a voice almost too beautiful to endure. It belongs to Aslan and it is his summons to the new world: the creation of Narnia. The music of his voice fills the children with joy, although they hardly understand what is happening. "But the Witch looked as if, in a way, she understood the music better than any of them," Lewis wrote. "Her mouth was shut, her lips pressed together, and her fists were clenched. Ever since the song began she had felt that this whole world was filled with a Magic different from hers and stronger. She hated it."[21]

In the worlds of Middle-earth and Narnia, evil is a perversion of goodness, which is the ultimate reality. Although Lewis is much more explicit in naming God as the source of everything good in the world, Tolkien shares his Christian belief that evil represents a rejection of God and the joy and beauty and virtue that originate in him.[22] Evil is a mutation, a parasite, an interloper. It is an ancient Darkness that fears and despises the Light. At war with the good, it is an immensely powerful force in human life and human societies. "If anguish were visible," Tolkien once explained, "almost the whole of this benighted planet would be enveloped in a dense dark vapor, shrouded from the amazed vision of the heavens!"[23]

The presence and power of evil is a dominant theme in Lewis's science-fiction trilogy. In the first novel, *Out of the Silent*

Planet (1938), we are introduced to Elwin Ransom, a middle-aged university professor who—like Lewis, also wounded in a war—is inclined to mind his own business. He is kidnapped by Dick Devine and Dr. Weston, a mad scientist who will stop at nothing to extend the human race to other planets. They travel to Malacandra (Mars), where we learn that the ruler of Thulcandra (Earth) became "bent" and "it was in his mind to spoil other worlds besides his own." But "a great war" between him and Maleldil, the ruler of the universe, left Earth estranged from the rest of the solar system.

Ransom's adventures continue in *Perelandra* and *That Hideous Strength*, in which the struggle to remake and subjugate the human race reaches a climax on planet Earth, in the English town of Edgestow. There a sinister force, embodied in the National Institute for Co-ordinated Experiments (N.I.C.E.), has taken root. Warns Ransom: "The Hideous Strength holds all this Earth in its fist to squeeze as it wishes."[24] It has drawn into its vortex Mark Studdock and his wife, Jane, who realize almost too late the nature of the threat. A struggle of cosmic proportions ensues. Not surprisingly, the abuse of science and technology lies near the heart of the contest. Wrote an early reviewer in *Punch* magazine: "It is Mr. Lewis's triumph to have shown, with shattering credibility, how the pitiful little souls of Jane and Mark Studdock become the apocalyptic battlefield of Heaven and Hell."[25]

When, in the 1930s, Tolkien and Lewis began to compose their stories, traditional belief in the existence of evil was already out of fashion. As we've seen, leaders in educated circles had dispensed with these "medieval" concepts as the vestiges of religious superstition. In our own day, the concept of evil remains perhaps the most controversial idea in any discussion about God, religion, or Christianity. Skeptics see a psychological tool to repress the members of a community or demonize those outside it. They have a point: no one who studies the history of the West could fail to note the abuse of religious doctrine for perverse ends.

Nevertheless, these authors anchor their stories in the ancient idea of the Fall of Man: just as a force of evil entered our world in a distant past, so it inhabits and threatens the worlds of their imaginations. It is the deepest source of alienation and conflict in their stories. Even so, it cannot erase the longing for goodness and joy, so palpably alive in the best and noblest of their characters. They are haunted by the memory of Eden: take away this fundamental idea, and their moral vision collapses.[26]

DESTINY AND FREE WILL

We might expect their stories, rooted in this belief, to lurch in one of two directions: either toward the triumphalism of the crusader, as we saw during the First World War; or toward fatalism, a cast of mind that renders men and women helpless victims in the storms of life. Instead, the heroes of Middle-earth and Narnia are much more complex. They are often hobbled by their own fears and shortcomings; they resist the burdens of war. Yet we also see in them an affirmation of moral responsibility—an irreducible dignity—even amid the terrible forces arrayed against them.

This tension appears repeatedly—relentlessly—in *The Lord of the Rings*, from its opening pages to its closing chapters. Immediately after Gandalf explains to Frodo that Sauron the Great, the Dark Lord, has arisen again and returned to Mordor to pursue his wicked designs, Frodo shrinks back. "I wish it need not have happened in my time," he says. "So do I," says Gandalf, "and so do all who live to see such times. But that is not for them to decide. All we have to decide is what to do with the time that is given us."[27]

When the Council gathers in Rivendell to determine how to destroy the Ring, Elrond reminds the Company that help will come from "other powers and realms that you know not." And yet, he warns, the road ahead will be very hard. "This quest may be attempted by the weak with as much hope as the strong. Yet such is oft the course of deeds that move the wheels of the world: small hands do them because they must, while the eyes of the great are elsewhere."[28]

Frodo is joined in his quest by his friends from the Shire: Sam, Merry, and Pippin. In addition to the hobbits, there is Aragorn, a Ranger of the North—a "hidden king" of Gondor—whose life is devoted to the war against Sauron; Legolas, king of the elves of Northern Mirkwood; and Gimli, a descendant of Gloin, a noble line of dwarves. Gandalf the Grey has joined them as well, their powerful protector and guide. But Gandalf becomes lost to them, dragged into an abyss by the Balrog at the Bridge of Khazad-Dum, and they are forced to flee for their lives. The loss pierces them with grief. "Frodo heard Sam at his side weeping, and then he found that he himself was weeping as he ran."[29]

Yet they carry on. They make their way to Caras Galadhon, home of Lady Galadriel, "the mightiest and fairest of all the Elves that remained in Middle-earth."[30] As they gather before her, she fixes her eyes on each of them and delivers a fierce warning: "Your Quest stands upon the edge of a knife. Stray but a little and it will fail, to the ruin of all."[31] What are they to do?

Tolkien's account of the condition of their hearts is as true to human life in the shadow of death as anything in modern prose. Each of them is faced with the appalling clarity of the choice laid before him: to continue in the quest, into dangers and horrors unspeakable, or to take the safe and easy way and turn back. "All of them, it seemed, had fared alike: each had felt that he was offered a choice between a shadow full of fear that lay ahead, and something that he greatly desired. Clear before his mind it lay, and to get it he had only to turn aside from the road and leave the Quest and the war against Sauron to others."[32]

The choice they face is also a summons; not a blind accident, but a Calling on their lives. One may answer the Call—or refuse it, turn away, and walk into Darkness. But indifference to the Call to struggle against evil is not an option; one must take sides. Thus, set before our imagination in the works of Tolkien and Lewis is one of the great paradoxes of our mortal lives: the mysterious intersection of providence and free will.[33]

Consider the exchange between Sam and Frodo as they rest for a moment along the stairs at Cirith Ungol, the cleft through the Western Mountains of Mordor. The area is heavily guarded by the Enemy. Forced to rely on the treacherous Gollum as their guide, they are anxious, weary, and short of food and water. Reflecting on their plight, Sam grows philosophical about the events that have brought them to this moment of danger, and the choices they have made along the way.

"I don't like anything here at all," said Frodo, "step or stone, breath or bone. Earth, air and water all seem accursed. But so our path is laid."

"Yes, that's so," said Sam. "And we shouldn't be here at all, if we'd known more about it before we started. But I suppose it's often that way. The brave things in the old tales and songs, Mr. Frodo: adventures, as I used to call them. I used to think that they were things the wonderful folk of the stories went out and looked for, because they wanted them, because they were exciting and life was a bit dull, a kind of sport, as you might say. But that's not the way of it with the tales that really mattered, or the ones that stay in the mind. Folk seem to have been just landed in them, usually—their paths were laid that way, as you put it. But I expect they had lots of chances, like us, of turning back, only they didn't."[34]

Here is a truth that Tolkien must have learned during the Great War, an "adventure" he did not seek out, but one that came to him, unwanted. *They had lots of chances, like us, of turning back, only they didn't.* This freedom to either fulfill or evade the Calling on one's life is central to Tolkien's work—and to his understanding of the human condition.

Like Tolkien, Lewis did not limit the need for painful choices to his main protagonists; most everyone is judged by the decisions he makes, or fails to make, when the Call to do battle arrives. In *The Magician's Nephew*, the Cabby and his wife, a humble couple from a modest part of London, have been chosen to rule Narnia as its first king and queen. They are warned that there will be challengers to their throne. What, Aslan asks, are they prepared to do?

"And if enemies came against the land (for enemies will arise) and there was war, would you be the first in the charge and the last in the retreat?"

"Well, sir," said the Cabby very slowly, "a chap don't exactly know till he's been tried. I dare say I might turn out ever such a soft 'un. Never did no fighting except with my fists. I'd try—that is, I 'ope I'd try—to do my bit."

"Then," said Aslan, "you will have done all that a King should do."[35]

We are led to believe that the choices of these characters—their decisions to put away fear and ego and choose goodness—are freely made and yet made with the help of a source of strength outside them. Tolkien was reluctant to name this power, though elsewhere he explained that "the religious element is absorbed into the story and the symbolism."[36] Thus, in *The Lord of Rings* we're told that Bilbo "was meant to find the Ring," that Frodo was "appointed" and "chosen" to carry it to Mordor, that even as the Fellowship decides its next move "the tides of fate are flowing." Destiny and free will are commingled throughout: "But you have been chosen," says Gandalf, "and you must therefore use such strength and heart and wits as you have."[37]

Lewis's use of allegory leaves no doubt about the Person who transcends the struggles of our earthly lives, even as he involves himself deeply in them. In *The Horse and His Boy*, Shasta and Aravis, helped by talking horses, race across the desert to warn Archenland and Narnia of the approaching army of Rabadash, bent on their destruction. Before reaching their goal they are attacked by a lion. Aravis, further behind, is moments from being cut down by the beast. Shasta faces a moment of decision:

"Stop," bellowed Shasta in Bree's ear. "Must go back. Must help!"

Shasta slipped his feet out of the stirrups, slid both his legs over the left side, hesitated for one hideous hundredth of a second, and jumped. It hurt horribly and nearly winded him; but before he knew how it hurt him he was staggering back to help

Aravis. He had never done anything like this in his life before and hardly knew why he was doing it now.[38]

The lion, we learn later, was Aslan in disguise. He is determined to guide the children in their journey, even if it means danger and suffering. Though Lewis provided us only with fragments of his wartime experience, we may imagine that, on at least one occasion, he found himself "staggering back to help" a friend under fire, hardly aware of what he was doing. Indeed, the scene would have been familiar to countless soldiers in the Great War, in every war that has ever been fought: the image of a soldier throwing himself into harm's way to rescue a fallen comrade.

POWER, SCIENCE, AND SEDUCTION

It is one thing to join a struggle against evil in the world, but it is another thing to persevere—to continue to resist the dark temptations inherent in the contest. It cannot be emphasized enough that the human tragedy of the First World War damaged the very idea of free will. After all, millions of men were flung into the pitiless machinery of a conflict that robbed them of their humanity. They were mutilated, bombed, bayoneted, gassed, and obliterated without mercy. The utter helplessness of the individual soldier on the Western Front was a recurring theme of postwar literature.

It is this very idea that Tolkien and Lewis repudiate throughout their works. In *The Fellowship of the Ring*, for example, we watch Frodo struggle to resist the almost overwhelming desire to use the Ring as the terror of the Dark Riders approaches. He yields to the temptation, and later reproaches himself bitterly: "for he now perceived that in putting on the Ring he obeyed not his own desire but the commanding wish of his enemies."[39] Though fighting his attackers furiously, he is stabbed with the deadly Morgul-knife, the poison of which would bring him under the power of the Dark Lord. Healed by his friends, he marvels at his escape. "Yes, fortune or fate have helped you," says Gandalf, "not to mention courage. For your heart was not touched, and only your shoulder was pierced; and that was because you resisted to the last."[40]

In Frodo we are meant to see ourselves: our weaknesses, our rationalizations, and our lack of resolve in combatting evil. But we also get a glimpse into a life of courage and perseverance in the ongoing struggle: *you resisted to the last*. Tolkien's story reminds us that evil is a sleepless force in human lives, and that the war against it demands constant vigilance.

After the Council of Elrond, when Frodo agrees to take the Ring to Mordor, he is confronted by Boromir, who has joined the Fellowship. Boromir is "a valiant man," a mighty warrior, but also a figure torn between honor and pride, power and wisdom.[41] He disagrees with the Council's decision to destroy the Ring, and accuses them of being timid rather than wise. "True-hearted Men, they will not be corrupted," he assures Frodo. His motives, he insists, are pure: "We do not desire the power of wizard-lords, only strength to defend ourselves, strength in a just cause," he says. "And behold! In our need chance brings to light the Ring of Power. . . . It is mad not to use it, to use the power of the Enemy against him."[42]

It all sounds so reasonable to modern ears. Yet it is Boromir, by turning on Frodo and forcing him to flee, who breaks the Fellowship and endangers them all. Boromir repents of his treachery, but it costs him his life.

For Saruman, a wizard originally committed to helping Middle-earth in its struggle against Sauron, his betrayal robs him of his soul. In his confrontation with Gandalf, he explains that "a new Power is rising" that cannot be openly resisted. The path of wisdom, he insists, is to join the Power and wait for an opportunity to alter its course. "As the Power grows, its proved friends will also grow; and the Wise, such as you and I, may with patience come at last to direct its courses, to control it," he says. "We can bide our time, we can keep our thoughts in our hearts, deploring maybe evils done by the way, but approving the high and ultimate purpose."[43]

Their noble aims would not change, we are assured, only the means to achieve them. This is the exact rationale offered by Nikabrik, one of the black dwarves in *Prince Caspian* who joins the Narnian resistance against the Telmarines. After the Narnians suffer many defeats, Nikabrik grows pessimistic. At a council of Caspian's advisors, they decide to blow the horn belonging to the ancient Queen Susan, to summon help from Aslan. When no help arrives, an embittered Nikabrik suggests it is time to turn elsewhere for aid:

> "Either Aslan is dead," said Nikabrik, "or he is not on our side. Or else something stronger than himself keeps him back. . . . You may drop Aslan out of the reckoning. I was thinking of someone else." There was no answer, and for a few minutes it was so still that Edmund could hear the wheezy and snuffling breath of the Badger.
>
> "Who do you mean?" said Caspian at last.
>
> "I mean a power so much greater than Aslan's that it held Narnia spellbound for years and years, if the stories are true."

"The White Witch!" cried three voices all at once. . . .

"Yes," said Nikabrik very slowly and distinctly, "I mean the Witch. Sit down again. Don't take fright at a name as if you were children. We want power: and we want a power that will be on our side."[44]

Nikabrik's ruthlessness, his willingness to compromise with evil, becomes his downfall. It is hard to imagine a more cautionary tale for the crusader in all of us: however noble the motives may be, they easily become twisted by the thought of glory and the taste of power.

For Tolkien and Lewis, it was a theme of utmost urgency. In the modern world, new technologies—what Winston Churchill called "the lights of perverted science"—were being used to extinguish human freedom. "The physical sciences, good and innocent in themselves, had already, even in Ransom's own time begun to be warped, had been subtly maneuvered in a certain direction," wrote Lewis in *That Hideous Strength*. "Despair of objective truth had been increasingly insinuated into the scientists; indifference to it, and concentration upon mere power, had been the result."[45]

The perverse relationship between technology, science, and power became a defining reality of the postwar years. Eugenics, communism, fascism, Nazism: these were the revolutions and ideologies that arose in the exhaustion of the democracies of Europe, all in the name of advancing the human race. All began by promising liberation from oppression; all became instruments of totalitarian control. "Dreams of the far future destiny of man," wrote Lewis, "were dragging up from its shallow and unquiet grave the old dream of Man as God."[46] As Tolkien biographer

Tom Shippey explains: "The major disillusionment of the twentieth century has been over political good intentions, which have led only to gulags and killings fields. That is why what Gandalf says has rung true to virtually everyone who reads it."[47]

THE DESCENT INTO DARKNESS

The power of evil is not confined to a single, swift decision to side with the Enemy. More often it involves a subtle and gradual perversion. This, in fact, is the burden of Tolkien's story: whether Frodo can resist the soul-destroying influence of the Ring and carry it to its final destination. Because of its great power, the Ring could be used to overthrow Sauron. Yet its power is conditioned to serve its evil maker, and "the very desire of it corrupts the heart." Elrond explains the inescapable dilemma: "And that is another reason why the Ring should be destroyed: as long as it is in the world it will be a danger even to the Wise. For nothing is evil in the beginning. Even Sauron was not so. I fear to take the Ring to hide it. I will not take the Ring to wield it."[48]

Near the moral center of *The Lord of the Rings* is the ancient problem of the Will to Power: the universal temptation to exploit, dominate, and control the lives of others. This is the motive force animating the great Enemy of Middle-earth. "But the only measure he knows is desire," says Gandalf, "desire for power."[49] Because Tolkien wrote his trilogy during and after the Second World War, when the world had entered the atomic age, many assumed that the story of the Ring was an allegorical warning about the horror of nuclear weapons. Tolkien set them straight: "Of course my story is not an allegory of Atomic power, but of *Power*," he said, "exerted for Domination."[50]

It may well be, as some scholars contend, that the "gathering darkness" over the remnants of the West in the Third Age of Middle-earth was propelled by the "gathering storm" of European fascism that threatened Western civilization in the 1930s and 1940s.[51] Two of Tolkien's sons, Christopher and Michael, became combatants in the Second World War, and his letters to them during this period contain numerous references to his own war experience. The uncertainties and terrors of a second global conflict in his lifetime undoubtedly worked upon his mind and energies.

Nevertheless, the appeal of Tolkien's work lies partly in the fact that contemporary events seemed to conform—tragically—to the pattern of human life expressed in its pages.[52] In this, Tolkien understood the problem not merely as the abuse of power: it was the temptation to pride, which the possession of power instigated and elevated into the fatal sin. "It was part of the essential deceit of the Ring," he explained, "to fill minds with imaginations of supreme power."[53] The possession of such power inevitably placed the unconstrained Self on the throne of the universe.

Much of the dramatic genius of *The Lord of the Rings* depends on the fact that none of its characters, not even its noblest, are immune to the danger; any of them might be tempted to betray themselves and their cause. "I have come," says Frodo, clutching the Ring at the brink of the chasm, at the Crack of Doom. "But I do not choose now to do what I came to do. I will not do this deed. The Ring is mine!" In the end, even Frodo—who sought with all his heart to avoid becoming the Ring-bearer—cannot resist its seductive power.[54]

Like Tolkien, Lewis was acutely conscious of the deceptive allure of power. A recurring motif of his works is how soft and subtle compromises can initiate a total corruption. "It does not matter how small the sins are provided that their cumulative effect is to edge the man away from the Light and out into Nothing," counsels the senior demon in Lewis's *The Screwtape Letters.* "Indeed the safest road to Hell is the gradual one—the gentle slope, soft underfoot, without sudden turnings, without milestones, without signposts."[55]

This insight is on magnificent display in *That Hideous Strength,* when Mark Studdock is first enticed by the wicked operatives of the N.I.C.E. They want Studdock to write a false news account of "riots" in Edgestow, which would give the Government an excuse to exercise emergency powers—and tighten its grip on the town. "But how are we to write it tonight if the thing doesn't even happen till tomorrow at the earliest?" he asks. His companions burst into laughter, and pour him another drink.

What comes next is a description of an ordinary man's descent into darkness, a scene no doubt repeated endlessly in the cultural chaos and revolutions following the Great War:

> This was the first thing Mark had been asked to do which he himself, before he did it, clearly knew to be criminal. But the moment of his consent almost escaped his notice; certainly there was no struggle, no sense of turning a corner. . . . But for him, it all slipped past in a chatter of laughter, of that intimate laughter between fellow professionals, which of all earthly powers is strongest to make men do very bad things before they are yet, individually, very bad men.[56]

This is why so much is made of Edmund's entrapment by the White Witch in *The Lion, the Witch, and the Wardrobe.* Aware that the children are a threat to her rule, she preys upon Edmund's weakness of character to betray them to her. How can Edmund—not an obviously wicked boy—be so blind to her machinations? The answer is a twofold desire: "Turkish Delight and to be a Prince." These become the obsessions of his life. Turkish Delight is Edmund's favorite sweet, and the White Witch uses it to bait him into her service. If he agrees, she leads him to believe, he can have all the Turkish Delight he craves. She will even make him a prince, allowing him to rule over his brother and sisters.

Edmund succumbs. He is to blame for his fall into temptation; he gives himself over to gluttony and his inclination to dominate others. Yet there is an outside power at work as well: unknown to Edmund, this was "enchanted Turkish Delight" and "anyone who had once tasted it would want more and more of it, and would even, if they were allowed, go on eating it till they killed themselves."[57] What Lewis was describing, of course, is an addiction, instigated by moral failure—a lust for pleasure and power.

A PSYCHOLOGY OF GOOD AND EVIL

The idea of personal moral guilt, however, was widely rejected in the postwar years. Psychology, philosophy, literature, even theology—all these disciplines were helping to erode individual responsibility. Vices and addictions were explained medically or scientifically, not in moral or religious terms. "Collective" or "biological" forces replaced old-fashioned notions of "sin."

As early as 1924, for example, attorney Clarence Darrow defended two Chicago men accused of murdering a boy in cold blood by making a novel claim. He insisted that criminal acts were the result of faulty evolution, not a faulty conscience. In his closing arguments, Darrow said the real question before the court was whether it would embrace "the old theory" that a person commits a criminal act "because he willfully, purposely, maliciously and with a malignant heart sees fit to do it," or the new scientific theory that "every human being is the product of the endless heredity back of him and the infinite environment around him."[58]

The denial of personal responsibility took a political turn as well. The outbursts of revolutionary violence rocking post-war Europe—the purges and assassinations in Lenin's Russia, for example—were rationalized as a necessary phase toward a utopian vision. An official of the Soviet Secret Police, the *Cheka*, explained thus: "We are not carrying out war against individuals. We are exterminating the bourgeoisie as a class."[59] As Paul Johnson writes, shortly after seizing power Lenin "abandoned the notion of individual guilt, and with it the whole Judeo-Christian ethic of personal responsibility."[60]

Tolkien and Lewis explicitly rejected these views as an assault on human freedom. The characters in their imaginative works are continually tested by the choices set before them. Each is involved in a great moral contest, a struggle against forces that would devour their souls. " 'It is very grievous,' said the Tisroc in his deep, quiet voice. 'Every morning the sun is darkened in my eyes, and every night my sleep is the less refreshing, because I remember that Narnia is still free.' "[61] Yet their characters retain the power of choice; there is nothing predetermined about the outcome. It is through their own decisions, their yielding to selfish ambitions, that they invite a spiritual crisis into their lives. The result is not the freedom they imagined, but the deepest slavery of heart and mind.

The mental outlook of Middle-earth and Narnia could hardly

be more out of step with the modern mind: here is an appeal to what might be called a "psychology of evil" as old as the story of Cain and Abel. It is the story of men and women given a birthright of freedom, but abusing their freedom for selfish ends. "Sin is crouching at your door," God warned Cain before he murdered his brother. "It desires to have you, but you must master it."[62]

Although Tolkien's work appears to lack a religious framework—there are no prayers or acts of worship, for example—its characters are conscious of a Moral Law, a source of Goodness to which they must give account.[63] The conflict between Mordor and Middle-earth occurs in a world of timeless moral truths, where men and women must choose sides in a titanic struggle between light and darkness. "How shall a man judge what to do in such times?" asks Éomer. Aragorn's response is unequivocal: "As he ever has judged," he says. "Good and ill have not changed since yesteryear; nor are they one thing among Elves and Dwarves and another among Men. It is a man's part to discern them." In his review of Tolkien's work, Lewis declared this to be "the basis of the whole Tolkienian world."[64]

Critics sometimes accuse the authors of creating black-and-white characters to personify their religious beliefs. But the careful reader sees something else entirely: individuals often at war with their own desires. The heroes of these stories are vulnerable to temptation and corruption, while the antagonists are almost never beyond redemption. Here, in fantasy and myth, no one escapes the long and harassing shadow of the biblical fall.

Indeed, a bedrock belief in evil, and in the responsibility to resist it, gives the writings of Tolkien and Lewis their dignity and power. It is the reason their stories, so fantastical in style, seem to speak into our present reality. The war against evil is the

moral landscape of *our* mortal lives: a journey of souls degraded or redeemed, dragged into the Darkness of self or led into the Light of grace.

THE REALISM OF FANTASY

As important as these themes are in the works of Tolkien and Lewis, we must not lose sight of the fact that they are embedded in a narrative of brutal, physical warfare. Narnia and Middle-earth are worlds embroiled in violent conflict—no less so than that of their authors during the years 1914–1918. Though considered romances, there is nothing romantic about the scenes of suffering depicted throughout.

The spectacle of human refugees was one of the defining features of the war. Paris experienced a mass exodus of civilians following the first bombardment of the city in August 1914. By September, about 700,000 people had left Paris, of whom 220,000 were children under the age of fifteen.[65] In October, after the Germans entered the Belgian port of Ostend, nearly all of Belgium fell under German occupation. Tens of thousands of refugees fled for England. Wrote Thomas Hardy:

> *Then I awoke; and lo, before me stood*
> *The visioned ones, but pale and full of fear;*
> *From Bruges they came, and Antwerp, and*
> *   Ostend. . . .*
> *Of ravaged roof, and smouldering gable-end.*[66]

Refugees would continue to pour from the cities, towns, and villages of Europe until the end of the war; the British and American armies encountered thousands of them during Germany's massive spring offensive of 1918. Thus Tolkien includes scenes of anguished refugees throughout his works. They appear in the form of Tuor and his family, who have escaped the ruined city in "The Fall of Gondolin." They are the villagers forced from Laketown by the death of Smaug in *The Hobbit*. In *The Lord of the Rings*, they are the folk of Westfold—"old and young, children and women"—hiding in the caves at Helm's Deep.[67] And they are the desperate inhabitants of Minas Tirith, escaping by wagon train for the southern hills before the Battle of Pelennor Fields.[68]

In *The Return of the King*, we read of the fierce, existential struggle between the forces of Mordor and the army of Gondor. It is the great battle of this great and vicious war, and its dead are too numerous to count. It leaves the victors "weary beyond joy or sorrow."[69] In his account of the contest at Pelennor Fields, Tolkien might well have been describing No Man's Land at the Somme:

> Then the Sun went at last behind Mindolluin and filled all the sky with a great burning, so that the hills and the mountains were dyed as with blood; fire glowed in the River, and the grass of the Pelennor lay red in the nightfall. And in that hour the great Battle of the field of Gondor was over; and not one living foe was left within the circuit of the Rammas.[70]

Later in the story, as Sam and Frodo pass through the Dead Marshes on their approach to Mordor, they enter a landscape deeply reminiscent of the battlefields in France and Belgium: the bomb-wracked craters swollen with water, filth, and the remains of the fallen; the painful whiff of mustard gas; the noxious stench of death. "The air, as it seemed to them, grew harsh, and filled with a bitter reek that caught the breath and parched their mouths," wrote Tolkien. "Here nothing lived, not even the leprous growths that feed on rottenness. The gasping pools were choked with ash and crawling muds, sickly white and grey, as if the mountains had vomited the filth of their entrails upon the lands about." Here, as at so many places along the Western Front, was a land desecrated and diseased beyond healing.[71]

There are great victories over the forces of darkness in *The Lord of the Rings*, but not without profound loss. There is determination, but it is often mixed with dread, with a burden of fear that all the efforts of the Fellowship will come to nothing.

Such is the lot of Merry and Pippin after being captured by the orcs and dragged off to their execution. They manage to escape, but remain in a state of constant danger. "No listener would have guessed from their words that they had suffered cruelly, and been in dire peril, going without hope towards torment and death," wrote Tolkien, "or that even now, as they knew well, they had little chance of ever finding friend or safety again."[72] Such also is the condition of otherwise stouthearted warriors as the hideous Nazgûl circle overhead. Like soldiers seeking refuge from a hail of mortar fire at Verdun, "they thought no more of war; but only of hiding and of crawling, and of death."[73]

Here is why Tolkien's work has been called a modern story, a "descent into hell" in its description of the sufferings of war.[74] Perhaps, in a sense, Tolkien has written a kind of war diary after all: an account of the pains and terrors of combat, yet clothed in the language of myth. "It might indeed be seen in certain respects as the last work of First World War literature," writes Brian Rosebury, "published almost forty years after the war ended."[75]

Because Lewis intended his Narnia stories for children, he

does not dwell on depictions of physical suffering, nor does he describe the corpses of the fallen in battle. Nevertheless, Lewis does not fully shield his readers from the brutalities of war. In *The Horse and His Boy*, at the fight at Anvard, Shasta is thrust into the battle. As the Calormene army approaches, the ground narrows between the two advancing armies, and the young and untested soldier is filled with fear. Lewis might have been remembering the moments before his own great test under fire, when he and his battalion went over the top of their trenches at Riez du Vinage: "All swords out now, all shields up to the nose, all prayers said, all teeth clenched," he wrote. "Shasta was dreadfully frightened. But suddenly it came into his head, 'If you funk this, you'll funk every battle all your life. Now or never.' "[76]

In *The Lion, the Witch, and the Wardrobe*, we read of Peter's first experience of combat, an encounter with a giant wolf. The creature turns on him with flaming, ferocious eyes, intent on tearing him apart. Putting aside his fear, Peter plunges his sword into its chest. "Then came a horrible, confused moment like something in a nightmare," Lewis wrote. "He was tugging and pulling and the Wolf seemed neither alive nor dead, and its bared teeth knocked against his forehead, and everything was blood and heat and hair." After drawing out his sword from the beast, Peter wipes the sweat off his face. "He felt tired all over."[77]

Lewis once admitted that his memories of war invaded his dreams for years: his account of Peter's battle could have been any soldier's recollection of bayoneting the enemy for the first time.

As in Tolkien's trilogy, Lewis's Narnia series depicts war not as an opportunity for martial glory, but as a grim necessity. When victories are won, there is a striking lack of triumphalism; we find instead amazement and gratitude for surviving the encounter. Battle scenes, though never lengthy, are described with surprising realism.

Edmund's contest against the White Witch, for example, might become the stuff of song and legend, but it left him shattered and bloody.[78] In *Prince Caspian*, Reepicheep is wounded so badly in battle that he seemed "little better than a damp heap of fur." The intrepid mouse is rendered "more dead than alive, gashed with innumerable wounds, one paw crushed, and, where his tail had been, a bandaged stump." There is hardly a more poignant reminder of suffering during the First World War than the images of soldier amputees, limping from a dugout or infirmary.

Likewise, the description of the battle between Caspian and the forces of Miraz redounds with the miscalculations and depredations of the combat soldier:

> At last there came a night when everything had gone as badly as possible, and the rain which had been falling heavily all day had ceased at nightfall only to give place to raw cold. . . . Poor Wimbleweather, though as brave as a lion, was a true Giant in that respect. He had broken out at the wrong time and from the wrong place, and both his party and Caspian's had suffered badly and done the enemy little harm. The best of the Bears had been hurt, a Centaur terribly wounded, and there were few in Caspian's party who had not lost blood. It was a gloomy company that huddled under the dripping trees to eat their scanty supper.[79]

The military blunders, the fruitless acts of bravery, the bone-chilling rain, the meager rations: there were many days and nights just like these along the Western Front. Imaginary beasts aside, such scenes could have been lifted from the journal of any front-line soldier. Like Tolkien, though, Lewis includes these images not for their own sake, but to provide the matrix for the moral and spiritual development of his characters: "Eustace stood with his heart beating terribly, hoping and hoping that he would be brave."[80] Indeed, the most compelling personalities in their stories face down their fears and find themselves transformed by the crisis of their age.

THE HEROIC QUEST

The evils of the Great War created many cynics and pacifists in the years after peace was established. For them, there could be nothing heroic about the folly of war. Yet, as veterans of this conflict, Tolkien and Lewis chose to remember not only its horrors and sorrows: they wanted to recall the courage, sacrifice, and the friendships that made it endurable.

Retrieving the medieval concept of the heroic quest—reinventing it for the modern mind—is one of the signal achievements of their work. Whether in epics such as *Beowulf* or romances like Malory's *Morte d'Arthur*, Tolkien and Lewis both found in medieval literature a set of motifs and ideals worth recalling.[81] More than that, they believed the genre offered a tonic for the spiritual malaise of the modern age. Biographer John Garth's judgment of Tolkien applies to Lewis as well: "He did not simply preserve the traditions that the war threatened, but reinvigorated them for his own era."[82]

Each of the installments in *The Chronicles of Narnia* is awash in these traditions. Narnia is a realm of kings and queens, where a code of honor holds sway, where knighthood is won or lost on the field of battle. "This is the greatest shame and sorrow that could have fallen on us," says the Prince in *The Silver Chair*. "We have sent a brave lady into the hands of enemies and stayed behind in safety."[83] The heroes of these stories—whether they take the form of princes or mice or Marsh-wiggles—are imbued with the medieval ideals of sacrifice and chivalry. "Sire, my life is ever at your command," pledges Reepicheep to Prince Caspian, "but my honor is my own."[84]

Tolkien once said that when he read a medieval work it stirred him to produce a modern work in the same tradition. This is what he has done in *The Lord of the Rings*.[85] As Verlyn Flieger observes, two of the central heroic figures of the story, Frodo and Aragorn, carry "a rich medieval heritage."[86] Yet in them Tolkien presents us with two kinds of heroes: the extraordinary man, the hidden king determined to fight for his people and regain his throne; and the ordinary man, the hobbit who, like many of us, is "not made for perilous quests" and prefers the comforts and safety of home.

In Aragorn we see the classic elements of the medieval knight: the casting of his broken sword upon the table at the Council of Elrond, his secret love for Arwen, his kingly leadership of the people of Gondor. Yet it is Aragorn's chivalrous character that holds the greatest appeal. His courage and ferocity in battle occur alongside his mercy and tenderness, especially toward the weak. His commitment to a just cause never devolves into a campaign for personal glory. "I am Aragorn son of Arathorn," he announces to Frodo and Sam, "and if by life or death I can save you, I will."[87]

At first glance, Frodo seems to have little in common with Aragorn. His is an orphan, with no kingly lineage. As a hobbit, he is small of stature, reticent by nature. He is no warrior. He views the burden of the Ring resentfully, and accepts it almost by accident. Yet in Tolkien's treatment, Frodo's character is deepened and enlarged by the trial he endures. He conquers his fears to face death against the Black Riders. He finds pity for the despicable Gollum. He battles the constant temptation of the Ring and summons the strength to press on, surprising even Gandalf with his courage. "My dear Frodo!" he exclaims. "Hobbits really are amazing creatures, as I have said before. You can learn all that there is to know about their ways in a month, and yet after a hundred years they can still surprise you at a pinch."[88]

In the aftermath of the First World War, there was deep cynicism about "the moralistic idealism" that created the slaughterhouse of the Western Front.[89] Modern liberalism had come to regard man's combative nature as an evil, and the chivalrous sentiment as the "false glamour" of war.[90] Even before the Enlightenment, of course, many Europeans (and Americans) had learned to despise the values associated with the medieval world. The forces of democracy, secularism, and feminism would discard them altogether.

No wonder critics accuse Tolkien and Lewis of forming a "cultural rearguard of the Middle Ages." Writes Lee Rossi: "They exhibit a tremendous nostalgia for the political stability and cultural cohesion of the Middle Ages."[91] In fact, neither sought a return to the political or social ideals of Christendom.[92] Nevertheless, they saw its tradition of valor and chivalry as both practical and vital. "It taught humility and forbearance to the great warrior," Lewis observed, "because everyone knew by experience how much he usually needed that lesson."[93]

Thus the noblest characters in their stories display gentleness as well as fierceness, the qualities embodied in the greatest knight in *Morte d'Arthur*: "Thou wert the meekest man that ever ate in hall among ladies; and thou wert the sternest knight to thy mortal foe that ever put spear in the rest." The heroes of Narnia and Middle-earth do not shrink from the sight of hacked-off limbs and smashed skulls; yet they also are men and women of great humility and modesty. The intended effect of these characters is to retrieve the medieval virtues and make them attractive, even to a modern audience.

Why did Tolkien and Lewis, ignoring the most powerful trends of their culture, embark on this task? Part of the answer lies in the battlefields of France. It was there, as young soldiers, that they encountered these virtues—in the officers and privates and medics at the Western Front. It was there, according to Tolkien, that the inspiration for his most beloved mythic character occurred. The exploits of the hobbits reveal how the "unforeseen and unforeseeable acts of will, and deeds of virtue of the apparently small, ungreat, forgotten in the places of the Wise and Great" shaped the destinies of nations.[94]

Rejecting equally the moods of militarism and pacifism, these authors charted a middle course: a partial return to the chivalrous ideal. Only a society that upheld this ideal—in its art, literature, and its institutions—could hope to resist the dark and hungry forces arrayed against it. The serene and pacific Rivendell is a vision, perhaps, of the world as it ought to be, but not as we actually find it. "There are in fact things with which it cannot cope," Tolkien said, "and upon which its existence nonetheless depends."[95] The heroic ideal in their stories is not escapism, they argued, but the only realistic path available in a dangerous world. As Lewis explained: "It offers the only possible escape from a world divided between wolves who do not understand, and sheep who cannot defend, the things which make life desirable."[96]

THE GIFT OF FRIENDSHIP

The heroic quest as understood by Tolkien and Lewis is unlike our modern notions of heroism in at least one other way: it is not a solitary endeavor. Students of war understand this truth better than most. Historian Stephen Ambrose introduced millions of readers to the importance of comradeship in wartime with his book *Band of Brothers*, the basis for the award-winning HBO miniseries. It is the story of the men of E Company, the 506th Regiment of America's 101st Airborne Division, from their initial training in 1942 to the end of the Second World War. "Within Easy Company they had made the best friends they had ever had, or would ever have," writes Ambrose. "They were prepared to die for each other; more important, they were prepared to kill for each other."[97]

This fact about the experience of combat was as relevant for the soldiers who went off to fight in 1914 as for those in 1939. The distance of that earlier war from our own time, the ruthlessness of the conflict, the ambiguity of its aims, its disastrous consequences for Western civilization—all these factors combine to prevent us from appreciating the intense sense of comradeship that shaped the lives of millions of young soldiers.

Yet for Tolkien and Lewis, their personal knowledge of the fellowship of men under fire must rank as another defining experience for their literary lives. As Lewis biographer Alan Jacobs observes, friendship is one of the most significant themes in *The Chronicles of Narnia*.[98] In *The Silver Chair*, we watch not only the growing friendship between Eustace and Jill Pole, but the stubborn loyalty of Puddleglum, as he decides to share the dangers of their quest: "Don't you lose heart, Pole," said Puddleglum. "I'm coming, sure and certain. . . . Now a job like this—a journey up north just as winter's beginning, looking for a prince who probably isn't there, by way of a ruined city that no one has ever seen—will be just the thing. If that doesn't steady a chap, I don't know what will."[99]

We see the cords of friendship develop between Aravis and Shasta in *The Horse and His Boy*, as the demands of war force them to work together, slowly replacing their resentments with deep admiration and, eventually, love. "In this idea about Aravis, Shasta was once more quite wrong," Lewis wrote. "She was proud and could be hard enough but she was as true as steel and would never have deserted a companion, whether she liked him or not."[100]

Indeed, it might be argued that friendship replaces romance as the preeminent expression of love in Lewis's stories. In *The Chronicles of Narnia* it flourishes between the children (the "sons and daughters of Adam"); between these children and the noble Narnians (the myriad of talking animals and mythological beasts); and, supremely, between Aslan, the great Lion, and all who serve him in love and obedience.[101] "To the Ancients, Friendship seemed the happiest and most fully human of all loves; the crown of life and the school of virtue," wrote Lewis. "The modern world, in comparison, ignores it."[102] In the world of Narnia—a realm ravaged by war—its essential role in human happiness is affirmed throughout.

Lewis first established friendships of this quality during the war years: with his brother, Warnie, whom he called "my dearest and closest friend," and in whom he found a confidant who understood the horrors of combat; with Laurence Johnson, who fought alongside him on the Western Front and shared his love of literature and philosophy; and with Edward "Paddy" Moore, who was sent to the Somme and with whom he made a pact to care for each other's family if either should be killed.[103] Years later, reflecting on the nature of friendship, Lewis turned naturally to the experience of war to explain what distinguished the love among friends from all other earthly loves:

> Every step of the common journey tests his metal; and the tests are tests we fully understand because we are undergoing them ourselves. Hence, as he rings true time after time, our reliance, our respect and our admiration blossom into an Appreciative love of a singularly robust and well-informed kind. If, at the outset, we had attended more to him and less to the thing our Friendship is "about," we should not have come to know or love him so well. You will not find the warrior, the poet, the philosopher or the Christian by staring into his eyes as if he were your mistress: better to fight beside him, read with him, argue with him, pray with him.[104]

We have seen how Tolkien was devoted to the friends of his school days, the men of the TCBS. In 1916, expecting to be sent soon into the theater of war, they held their own war meeting, "the Council of London." There they spoke of the ideas that moved them deeply, and pledged to support one another through the storms of war. When Tolkien enlisted with the 19th Lancashire Fusiliers, he hoped, like Lewis, to be going into combat with one of his closest friends.[105]

It is no accident, of course, that Tolkien called the first book of his trilogy *The Fellowship of the Ring*. Part of the immense attraction of the story is watching a contentious assemblage of hobbits, dwarves, and elves put away their differences and fight alongside one another against each new threat and danger. They begin their quest as reluctant allies, suspicious and even distrustful. Before it is complete—and after facing many terrors and setbacks—they are transformed into a fellowship of the noblest kind.

At the start of their journey, Elrond advises the Company that each may continue only as far as he chooses; none are under obligation to help the Ring-bearer all the way to Mount Doom. Gimli is quick to respond: "Faithless is he that says farewell when the road darkens." When Frodo arrives at Crickhollow, before setting out into the Old Forest, he is determined to leave on his own; he does not want to expose his companions to the perils that lie ahead. But Merry, Pippin, and Sam are wise to his plans and confront him before he can slip away. They insist on coming with him. Frodo, deeply moved, nevertheless protests. "But it does not seem that I can trust anyone." Merry is unflappable:

> "It all depends on what you want. You can trust us to stick to you through thick and thin—to the bitter end. And you can trust us to keep any secret of yours—closer than you keep it yourself. But you cannot trust us to let you face trouble alone, and go off without a word. We are your friends, Frodo. Anyway, there it is. We know most of what Gandalf has told you. We know a good deal about the Ring. We are horribly afraid—but we are coming with you; or following you like hounds."[106]

As vital as the Fellowship of the Ring is to Tolkien's story, the bond of friendship between Sam Gamgee and Frodo Baggins is one of the great triumphs of the work, inspired, as we have seen, by the rugged service of the batmen and soldiers in the trenches along the front. Like no other, Sam is the friend who would "jump down a dragon's throat" to save Frodo, "if he did not trip over his own feet."[107] Tolkien once called Sam "this jewel among the hobbits."[108]

Sam's loyalty is tested from beginning to end, from the decision to leave the Shire to the final approach to Mordor. "It is going to be very dangerous, Sam. It is already dangerous," warns Frodo. "Most likely neither of us will come back." Sam doesn't flinch: "If you don't come back, sir, then I shan't, that's certain. 'Don't you leave him!' they said to me. 'Leave him!' I said. 'I never mean to. I am going with him, if he climbs to the Moon; and if any of those Black Riders try to stop him, they'll have Sam Gamgee to reckon with.' "[109]

When Frodo and Sam are at the threshold of Mount Doom, near the very end of their quest, they find themselves nearly without strength to carry on. For Frodo there was "no taste of food, no feel of water, no sound of wind, no memory of tree or grass or flower." The desolation of the landscape, the black skies, the noxious fumes, the ash and slag and burned stone, and the dark slopes of the Mountain towering over them are almost overwhelming. They stagger toward their goal. Frodo, weakened by the great burden of carrying the Ring, begins to crawl on his hands.

> Sam looked at him and wept in his heart, but no tears came to his dry and stinging eyes. "I said I'd carry him, if it broke my back," he muttered, "and I will!"
>
> "Come, Mr. Frodo!" he cried. "I can't carry it for you, but I can carry you and it as well. So up you get! Come on, Mr. Frodo dear! Sam will give you a ride. Just tell him where to go, and he'll go."[110]

It is a good bet that only men who knew friendships of this kind—who experienced them on the field of combat—could write passages of such compassion, grit, and courage. After the war, Tolkien and Lewis sought to recapture something like the camaraderie that sustained them during the crisis years of 1914–1918. At Oxford they launched the Inklings, the group of friends and fellow scholars who met weekly—Tuesday mornings at the Eagle and Child pub over beer and Thursday evenings in Lewis's college rooms over various drinks—to discuss their works.[111]

For sixteen years these men gathered to read, recite, argue, and laugh together. They met faithfully, even during the darkest days of the Second World War. As Tolkien put it in a letter dated September 23, 1944: "The Inklings have already agreed that their victory celebration, if they are spared to have one, will be to take a whole inn in the country for at least a week, and spend it entirely in beer and talk, without any reference to a clock!"[112] Lewis read aloud many of his most important works during these gatherings. "What I owe them is incalculable," he acknowledged. "Is any pleasure on earth as great as a circle of Christian friends by a good fire?"[113]

During the course of four decades, Tolkien and Lewis became devoted to each other's success. Tolkien, through long talks and late evenings, played a crucial role in Lewis's conversion to Christianity. He helped Lewis find a publisher for his first novel, and was a major force in securing his appointment to the Chair of English at Magdalene College, Cambridge, in 1954, after Oxford denied him a professorship.

At the same time, the author of *The Hobbit* and *The Lord of the Rings* could have had no greater advocate for his imaginative works. Lewis even nominated Tolkien for the Nobel Prize in Literature. "C. S. Lewis is a very old friend and colleague of mine, and indeed I owe to his encouragement the fact that in spite of obstacles (including the 1939 war!) I persevered and eventually finished *The Lord of the Rings*," Tolkien wrote. "He heard all of it, bit by bit, read aloud."[114]

When Lewis learned that *The Lord of the Rings* had been accepted for publication, he wrote to Tolkien to describe his "sheer pleasure of looking forward to having the book to read and re-read." And then he added a most remarkable perspective on the importance of the book to both their lives: "But a lot of other things come in. So much of your whole life, so much of our joint life, so much of the war, so much that seemed to be slipping away quite *spurlos* [without trace] into the past, is now, in a sort made permanent."[115]

Such was the quality of their friendship: As with no one else, Tolkien dared to expose one of the great passions of his life, the construction of his epic trilogy, to the critical eyes of his friend and colleague. Lewis, for his part, became wholly invested in the project. Perhaps only Lewis, a soldier like Tolkien in the Great War, could recognize how his story "made permanent" their shared experience of the suffering and heartache of the war.[116]

Against the temper of their times, these authors dared to reclaim some of the older beliefs and virtues. Their common Christian faith had much to do with this, but perhaps no more so than their mutual love of mythic and romantic literature. As Lewis described it, they were "both soaked" in Homer, *Beowulf*, Norse mythology, medieval romance, and George MacDonald's fairy tales.[117] The result was a bond of loyalty and comradeship that transformed both their lives. "Friendship makes prosperity more shining," wrote Cicero, "and lessens adversity by dividing and sharing it."

Their experience reminds us that great friendship is a gift born of adversity: it is made possible by the common struggle against the world's darkness. "Most gracious host, it was said to me by Elrond Halfelven that I should find friendship upon the way, secret and unlooked for," Frodo tells Faramir. "*Certainly I have looked for no such friendship as you have shown. To have found it turns evil to great good.*"[118]

Though their friendship experienced periods of frustration and strain, it persevered to the end. "This feels like an axe-blow near the roots," Tolkien wrote after Lewis's death in November 1963. "We owed each a great debt to the other, and that tie, with the deep affection that it begot, remained."[119] Given the contemporary infatuation with "virtual" relationships, Tolkien and Lewis's achievement not only remains but continues to grow in stature. Like few other writers over the past century, they show us what friendship can look like when it reaches for a high purpose and is watered by the streams of sacrifice, loyalty, and love.

PLAYING OUR PART IN THE STORY

We have come to neglect this aspect of war. We understand its atrocities, its injustices, its heartbreak, and its horrors well enough. We rightly seek to avoid it, at almost any cost. But Tolkien and Lewis were not satisfied with this version of war.

They assumed that war would sometimes be necessary to preserve human freedom. "Give me the Narnian wars where I shall fight as a free Horse among my own people!" says Shasta. "Those will be wars worth talking about."[120] They believed that a "Hideous Strength" roamed the earth: a force of evil that sought to destroy human societies. Its perpetual war within and against the souls of men would make peace impossible—impossible, at least, for those who wished to live in freedom. "The soil of the

Shire is deep," explains Merry in *The Return of the King*. "Still there are things deeper and higher; and not a gaffer could tend his garden in what he calls peace, but for them."[121]

Such knowledge allowed these authors to look at human life, caught in the calamity of a global conflict, without illusions. Indeed, the heroic ideal in their works is made more poignant by their awful realism: in the struggle against evil, the outcome is not assured. "War is upon us and all our friends, a war in which only the use of the Ring could give us surety of victory," says Gandalf. "It fills me with great sorrow and great fear: for much shall be destroyed and all may be lost."[122] *All may be lost.* By introducing and sustaining the real possibility of defeat, Tolkien and Lewis draw us into their epic dramas.

No matter how desperate the circumstances, however, the characters in their stories retain the capacity to resist evil and choose the good. Their moral and spiritual growth depends on whether or not they honor these obligations. "The individual exists in a realm where choice is always necessary," writes Patricia Meyer Spacks. "The freedom of that choice, for the virtuous, is of paramount importance."[123] As veterans of the most destructive war the word had ever seen, Tolkien and Lewis could not glorify its violence and anguish. But neither could they accept the fatalism and cynicism that had become so prevalent. Wilfred Owen's raging anthem against war—"the shrill, demented choirs of wailing shells"—could not be the final word.[124]

During the Second World War, Tolkien received a letter from his son Christopher, then serving with the Royal Air Force. Sensing his son's anxieties, he confessed that he knew the feeling of being "the toad under the harrow," conscripted into a deadly conflict, with fierce enemies all about. "Well, there you are: a hobbit amongst the Urukhai. Keep up your hobbitry in heart, and think that all *stories* feel like that when you are *in* them," he wrote. "You are inside a very great story!"[125]

The most influential Christian authors of the twentieth century believed that every human soul was caught up in a very great story: a fearsome war against a Shadow of Evil that has invaded the world to enslave the sons and daughters of Adam. Yet those who resist the Shadow are assured that they will not be left alone; they will be given the gift of friendship amid their struggle and grief. Even more, they will find the grace and strength to persevere, to play their part in the story, however long it endures and wherever it may lead them.

CONCLUSION

The Return of the King

The last soldier to die in the Great War was an American, twenty-three-year-old Henry Gunther, a private with the American Expeditionary Force in France. He was killed at 10:59 a.m., November 11, 1918, one minute before the Armistice went into effect.

Gunther's squad, part of the 79th Infantry Division, encountered a roadblock of German machine guns near the village of Chaumont-devant-Damvillers. Against the orders of his sergeant, he charged the guns with his bayonet. German soldiers, aware of the Armistice, tried to wave him off. But Gunther kept coming and was gunned down; he died instantly. His divisional record states: "Almost as he fell, the gunfire died away and an appalling silence prevailed."[1]

Despite the jubilation, the celebrations, the parties and parades marking the end of the First World War, a brutal silence fell over much of the world. It was the stillness of souls anguished and bewildered by the carnage of war. Poet Thomas Hardy, writing upon the signing of the Armistice, undoubtedly spoke for many:

> *Some could, some could not, shake off misery;*
> *The Sinister Spirit sneered: "It had to be!"*
> *And again the Spirit of Pity whispered, "Why?"*[2]

Like other young writers of their generation, Tolkien and Lewis sought to make sense of a conflict that claimed so much in blood and treasure and delivered so little to the cause of human happiness. "The Great War was a process by which all the great powers, victors and vanquished alike, transformed themselves from bastions of prosperity into sinkholes of poverty and debt," writes G. J. Meyer in *A World Undone*. "Financially as in so many other ways, the war was a road to ruin."[3] To some extent, Tolkien and Lewis were swept along this ruinous road: the realization that the prewar beliefs in mankind's inevitable progression, in the creation of something like heaven on earth, were cruelly mistaken.

Indeed, the Will to Power remained a permanent feature of the human predicament. The struggle between Good and Evil would not be resolved within human history. What, then, was the basis for hope?

WHEN HOPE VANISHES

There are moments in their stories, it must be said, when hope is virtually extinguished. In *The Last Battle*, Shift the Ape, a servant of Rishda Tarkaan, and the Calormenes have conquered Narnia. By creating "Tashlan," a confusion of Aslan with the demon Tash, they threaten to deceive even the most loyal followers of the lion.

Truth is rendered a useless weapon against their falsehood. As biographer Walter Hooper explains, this is not the wickedness we expect in an adventure story, but rather "a new and dreadful dimension where ordinary courage seems helpless."[4]

Dreadful indeed. As he lay dying after defending Narnia, Roonwit the Centaur delivers this message: ". . . remember that all worlds draw to an end and that noble death is a treasure which no one is too poor to buy."[5] Lewis is insistent on this point—that despite all our effort and sacrifice, even to the point of death, we cannot prevent a final defeat. The present world, always in the grip of Darkness, can never evolve into an earthly paradise. Rather, it will draw to a sudden and violent close: "an extinguisher popped on the candle, a brick flung at the gramophone, a curtain run down on the play."[6]

Tolkien likewise declines to offer a sweet and easy resolution to humanity's struggle with evil. Writing again to his son Christopher during the Second World War, he lamented "the appalling destruction and misery" of war. "There seem no bowels of mercy or compassion, no imagination, left in this dark diabolic hour."[7] The bitter realism of *The Lord of the Rings* is what makes the book so irresistibly relevant to our own situation. Not unlike Tolkien's postwar generation, we tend to be cynical about the ideals of an earlier time and the panaceas offered for our modern problems.

When Tolkien's characters are nearly broken by grief, by fear of losing all they hold dear, we cannot help but grieve with them. Think of the exchange between Éowyn and Faramir as they recover from their wounds in battle and wait with deep anxiety while the war for Middle-earth rages. As they look east, they see a "vast mountain of darkness" rising up and seemingly ready to engulf the whole world. "Then you think that the Darkness is coming?" says Éowyn. "Darkness Unescapable?"[8]

By the end of his quest, Frodo the Ring-bearer has given up the thought of survival. He has resigned himself to a final defeat: one of the brutal facts about the world as we find it. "Hope fails. An end comes," he tells Sam. "We have only a little time to wait now. We are lost in ruin and downfall, and there is no escape."[9]

For all the accusations of "medieval escapism," Tolkien comes closer to capturing the tragedy of the human condition than any postmodern cynic. At the climax of his journey, at the fires of Mount Doom, despite all his courage and strength, Frodo fails in his quest: he chooses not to destroy the Ring, but instead succumbs to its power and places it once again on his finger. "But one must face the fact," Tolkien wrote, "the power of Evil in the world is not finally resistible by incarnate creatures, however 'good.' "[10]

Here is where Tolkien and Lewis depart most radically from the spirit of the age. Our modern tales of heroism—the gallery of superheroes, super cops, and super spies—offer a protagonist who invariably saves the day by his (or her) natural intelligence and strength of will, usually with lots of firepower at hand. The idea that the hero would need outside help—from a supernatural deity, for example—strikes many as a cheat. It robs human beings of their "dignity" and diminishes "the human spirit." In the *Star Wars* franchise, the nebulous "Force" that aids Luke Skywalker in his struggle against Lord Vader even now seems quaint, out of date. We prefer Batman in *The Dark Knight Rises*, the brooding, obsessive figure who overcomes his demons to rescue Gotham more or less on his own. (Even Bruce Wayne's faithful butler, Alfred, disappears for most of the movie.)

The heroic ideal in the works of Tolkien and Lewis, however, is qualified in a much more profound way. The hero cannot, by his own efforts, prevail in the struggle against evil. The forces arrayed against him, as well as the weakness within him, make victory impossible. The tragic nature of his quest begins to dawn on him, to oppress him, until the moment when failure seems inevitable.

OVERCOMING CATASTROPHE

The mythic dimension of their stories now reaches its zenith: like the best fairy tales, they provide the consolation of the happy ending, "the sudden joyous turn" toward rescue and redemption. It is the reversal of a catastrophe, what Tolkien calls the *eucatastrophe*, a decisive act of Grace that promises to overcome our guilt, restore what has been lost, and set things right.[11]

Frodo fails in his quest. And yet his quest is accomplished, not by him, but by the most unlikely of creatures: Gollum. "His malice is great and gives him a strength hardly to be believed in one so lean and withered," says Gandalf. "But he may play a part yet that neither he nor Sauron have foreseen."[12] The wizard's prophecy is fulfilled. Frodo's defeat—our defeat—is overturned by a Power stronger than our weakness. Tolkien identified this Power as "that one ever-present Person who is never absent and never named."[13] So it is that Gollum, driven by his lust to dominate, bites off Frodo's finger that bears the Ring, only to slip and plunge to his death in the fire. The Ring is destroyed, not by Frodo or by the Fellowship, but by "a sudden and miraculous grace."[14]

In the Narnia series, this act of Grace first appears in *The Lion, the Witch, and the Wardrobe*. Edmund's betrayal of Aslan and his siblings has come at a great cost. "You know that every traitor belongs to me as my lawful prey," sneers the White Witch, "and that for every treachery I have a right to a kill." But Aslan intervenes. He offers his own life for Edmund's, allowing himself to be killed upon the Stone Table with the Stone Knife. Yet death cannot hold him, and the Lion returns to life and defeats the White Witch and all her forces. This is the "Deep Magic" that was put into the world by the Emperor-beyond-the-Sea: that when a willing victim, free of guilt, exchanges his life for that of a traitor, then "Death itself would start working backwards."[15]

The crowning moment of Grace occurs in *The Last Battle*, as King Tirian, the children, and a faithful remnant of Narnians fight their way to the entrance of the Stable: the last battle of the last King of Narnia. We are led to believe that inside the Stable is certain death, the stronghold of an all-powerful evil. "I feel in my bones," says Poggin, "that we shall all, one by one, pass through that dark door before morning. I can think of a hundred deaths I would rather have died."[16] As the company is forced inside its doors, all hope seems lost.

Here again comes the "joyous turn." The great Lion has invaded the Stable, cast out the demon Tash, and turned the Stable into a portal to Aslan's Country. The children watch as Narnia is destroyed and a new world, nearly more beautiful than their hearts can bear, is called into being. "All the old Narnia that mattered, all the dear creatures, have been drawn into the real Narnia through the Door."[17] Lucy captures the simple yet powerful symbolism of the Stable: in the Christian story, it is the birthplace of the Messiah, the Lion of the tribe of Judah, of Jesus the Christ. "In our world too, a Stable once had something inside it that was bigger than our whole world."[18]

These epic tales of heroism and sacrifice are strangely familiar to us because we have heard them, or rumors of them, before.

They are the stories of men and women overcome by evil, yet loved and redeemed by Grace. They are tales "held together by a central myth that manages to partake of all the myths of all the heroes of the past."[19] As manifestations of *eucatastrophe*, they point us toward that essential myth that Tolkien and Lewis once debated into the early morning hours at Oxford, the Myth that became Fact.

OUR INCONSOLABLE SECRET

Only after all the fighting is done, when the bravest have fallen in battle, when the war against evil has been fought to its bitter end— only after all this—does the Myth as Fact complete the human story. Only then can joy, "joy beyond the walls of the world," become our permanent possession.[20] There is no shortcut to the Land of Peace, no primrose path to the Mansions of the Blessed. First come tears and suffering in Mordor, heartless violence at Stable Hill—and horror and death at Golgotha.

Perhaps this is why the *eucatastrophe* is always mixed with grief: the knowledge of the sorrows endured in the struggle against evil lingers on in the human heart. "And all the host laughed and wept, and in the midst of their merriment and tears the clear voice of the minstrel rose like silver and gold, and all the men were hushed." And the minstrel sang to them, and he kept singing, "until their hearts, wounded with sweet words, over-flowed, and their joy was like swords, and they passed in thought to regions where pain and delight flow together and tears are the very wine of blessedness."[21]

The mingling of grief and joy, so descriptive of our mortal lives, is a recurring theme in the Bible. It is the experience of the

Jews in the days of Ezra the prophet: the knowledge of the presence of God after many years of spiritual famine. Returning from bitter years of war and captivity, they begin to rebuild the temple of the Lord—their house of worship that had been destroyed by Israel's enemies, initiating a long descent into slavery and exile. "And all the people gave a great shout of praise to the LORD, because the foundation of the house of the LORD was laid," wrote the prophet. "But many of the older priests and Levites and family heads, who had seen the former temple, wept aloud when they saw the foundation of this temple being laid, while many others shouted for joy."[22]

The conclusion of the Great War brought its own mix of celebration and sadness. The soldiers of this war had lived through endless days of mud, stench, slaughter, and death. Nothing like it had ever occurred in the history of the world; it shook the very foundations of civilized life.

"The Great War differed from all ancient wars in the immense power of the combatants and their fearful agencies of destruction, and from all modern wars in the utter ruthlessness with which it was fought," wrote Winston Churchill. "All the horrors of all the ages were brought together, and not only armies but whole populations were thrust into the midst of them."[23] Promises of swift victory were replaced by plans for a final "breakthrough" assault, which always ended in stalemate. It was a war that some feared might go on forever. "Whenever one side produced an implement of destruction that promised to tip the scales," writes G. J. Meyer, "the other came up with a way to preserve the deadlock."[24]

No wonder one newspaper called the Armistice "the greatest day in the history of the world."[25] There was rejoicing on that day, amid the oceans of sorrow.

Yet no full and final consolation could be found in the peace that followed. No war could end war for all time, or transform the nations into a brotherhood of man. "It was a loathsome ending to the loathsome tragedy of the last four years," wrote Siegfried Sassoon in his diary.[26] T. S. Eliot saw the postwar world as a wasteland of human weariness. "I think we are in rats' alley," he wrote, "where the dead men lost their bones."[27] Erich Remarque predicted a generation of men "broken, burnt out, rootless, and without hope." Civilian life, he said, would bring no comfort to the survivors: "We will not be able to find our way any more."[28]

BEHOLD THE KING

After returning to England from the front, Tolkien and Lewis might easily have joined the ranks of the rootless and disbelieving. Instead, they became convinced there was only one truth, one singular event, that could help the weary and brokenhearted find their way home: the Return of the King.

This King is stronger than "that Hideous Strength" that roams Narnia and Middle-earth looking for victims to devour. He is the archetype of the heroic, in every culture and in every age. He is the source of all goodness and courage, the desire of the nations. He comes to restore "the long-lost days of freedom."[29] This King alone knows the way to that Blessed Realm that lies beyond the Sea. "The light ahead was growing stronger," wrote Lewis in *The Last Battle*. "Lucy saw that a great series of many-colored cliffs led up in front of them like a giant's staircase. And then she forgot everything else, because Aslan himself was coming, leaping down from cliff to cliff like a living cataract of power and beauty."[30]

This King comes with power and beauty, as the voice of

conscience and the source of consolation, as the Lion and the Lamb. Here, perhaps, is the lingering influence of George MacDonald. "Loving-kindness beamed from every line of his face," he wrote of the noble knight in *Phantastes*. Even so, the knight's face grew "stern and determined, all but fierce," as his eyes "burned on like a holy sacrifice, uplift on a granite rock."[31] What Lewis discovered and came to embrace in MacDonald's vision was the "union of tenderness and severity."[32]

No character in all of Lewis's fiction embodies this blending of virtues more convincingly than Aslan. In *The Silver Chair*, Jill finds herself torn between fear and desire when the Lion appears and blocks her path to a stream of life-giving water:

> "Are you thirsty?" said the Lion.
>
> "I'm dying of thirst," said Jill.
>
> "Then drink," said the Lion. . . .
>
> "Will you promise not to—do anything to me, if I do come?"
>
> "I make no promise," said the Lion.
>
> "Do you eat girls?" she said.
>
> "I have swallowed up girls and boys, women and men, kings and emperors, cities and realms," said the Lion. It didn't say this as if it were boasting, nor as if it were sorry, nor as if it were angry. It just said it. . . .
>
> "Oh dear!" said Jill, coming another step nearer. "I suppose I must go and look for another stream then."
>
> "There is no other stream," said the Lion.[33]

In his youthful atheism, Lewis didn't recognize these qualities as belonging to the central figure of Christianity: Jesus the

Christ. But his own careful reading of the gospels helped change his mind. "Nowhere else outside the New Testament," he wrote, "have I found terror and comfort so intertwined."[34]

Tolkien achieves much the same effect with Aragorn, the chief epic hero of *The Lord of the Rings*. He is a man of great courage, determination, and humility. Aragorn carries several names, all rich in meaning. He first appears as Strider, a dark and mysterious traveler. As a child he was called Estel, a name meaning "hope," and a frequent theme throughout. In the House of Healing he names himself Envinyatur, or "Renewer." He is later called Lord of the Western Lands and King of the West. His true stature is revealed only after Sauron is defeated and he finally assumes his throne:

> But when Aragorn arose all that beheld him gazed in silence, for it seemed to them that he was revealed to them now for the first time. Tall as the sea-kings of old, he stood above all that were near; ancient of days he seemed and yet in the flower of manhood; and wisdom sat upon his brow, and strength and healing were in his hands, and a light was about him. And then Faramir cried: "Behold the King!"[35]

In the end, the creators of Narnia and Middle-earth offer a vision of human life that is at once terrifying and sublime. They insist that every soul is caught up in an epic story of sacrifice and courage and clashing armies: the Return of the King. It is the day when every heart will be laid bare. We will know, with inexpressible joy or unspeakable sorrow, whether we have chosen Light or Darkness. "For the day of the LORD is near," wrote the prophet, "in the valley of decision."[36] Hence comes a warning, as well as a blessing: to deny the King, to turn away in grief or rage, means endless ruin. But to behold him—to be counted among his Beloved—is to pass into life everlasting.

"Is everything sad going to come untrue?" asks Sam.[37] Here we find, beyond all imagination, the deepest source of hope for the human story. For when the King is revealed, "there will be no more night."[38] The Shadow will finally and forever be lifted from the earth. The Great War will be won.

This King, who brings strength and healing in his hands, will make everything sad come untrue.

ACKNOWLEDGMENTS

No book—at least no book by this author—can be written without the help of many hands and minds and voices. I want to thank my extended Italian-American family, whose love and support help sustain me. Special thanks to my brother, Mike, for his research into our family history and our mutual interest in the First World War, and to his wife, Ann Marie; to my sister Sue and her husband Joe, who lighten my burdens in so many ways; and to my nephews and niece, who remind me of what's really important. Many thanks to my cohort of friends and advisers, including: Kara Callaghan, Cherie Harder, John and Kelli Baker, Ken and Marilyn Jackson, Mark and Patti Kreslins, Lia and Charles Howard, Nile Gardiner, Pete Peterson, Fred Ferrara, Eric Metaxas, Alan Crippen, Mark Tooley, Jedd Medefind, Tim Schwartz, Charlie Catlett, Tim Montgomerie, Ben Rogers, Daniel Johnson, Os Guinness, and Michael Cromartie.

My research assistant, Carol Anne Kemp, a former student of mine at the King's College, deserves special recognition. Carol Anne's love and knowledge of the works of Tolkien and Lewis proved to be utterly indispensable. Her literary instincts—shared during our many conversations over coffee—improved the manuscript immeasurably.

Every historian owes a debt to those who have come before him. Many thanks to the Tolkien and Lewis scholars who have done so much to illuminate the lives of these great men, and to the Tolkien and Lewis estates for preserving their works. I am equally grateful to the many WWI historians who have devoted much of their professional lives to helping us understand the nature of that conflict.

I want to thank my friends at Thomas Nelson, Nelson Books: Joel Miller, for his robust support for the book before he moved on to other endeavors; Webster Younce, executive editor, for his strong encouragement; Janene MacIvor, senior editor, whose skill and patience and encouragement are without equal in the editing world; and copy editor Zachary Gresham, for his professionalism and dogged efforts. My literary agents, Joel Kneedler and Bryan Norman, also deserve much thanks.

I am also deeply grateful to Greg Thornbury, president of the King's College, for creating the space in my academic calendar to tackle the book, and for his great friendship, a tonic for the heart. I also want to thank all my colleagues and students at the King's College for their steady encouragement. Finally, many thanks to my friends at the District Church in Washington DC, especially members of the Lewis and Linguine group, for their fellowship in the faith.

A REMEMBRANCE

O ne of the great satisfactions of working on this book was learning more about how the First World War affected the lives of ordinary soldiers and their families—including my own family history.

My paternal grandfather, Michele (Michael) Loconte, was a twenty-year-old Italian émigré living and working in the United States when war broke out in August 1914. He was drafted into the US military in 1917 as America prepared to enter the war. After training with the 91st Division—known as the "Wild West Division"—he was deployed with the US Expeditionary Force to the Western Front in the summer of 1918. My grandfather served as a private with the 91st Division, C Company, the 316th Ammunition Train for the remainder of the war.

Beginning on September 20, 1918, Loconte's division participated in the Meuse-Argonne Offensive, the final and decisive campaign of the war—and the deadliest for the United States. More than 26,000 US soldiers were killed in the battle, including 1,702 from the 91st Division. The divisional record describes their advance during the last week of September:

During our march forward we had passed column after column of troops of other divisions and interminable truck trains had rumbled all night through every billeting town that we occupied. And now, hidden in the Foret de Hesse, we began to be surrounded by an ever-thickening concentration of artillery, long-range rifles, stumpy howitzers, battery after battery of smaller guns. They came in night after night, and by daybreak each new increment had melted out of sight in the woods and high roadside hedges, or had disappeared under camouflage in the open. It seemed as if all the guns in France were gathered together in the crowded forest.[1]

Their orders were unambiguous: they were to devote themselves unreservedly to the task of defeating the Germany army. "Divisions will advance independently of each other," the divisional record states, "pushing the attack with utmost vigor and regardless of cost."[2]

Although my grandfather rarely spoke about his wartime experience, he must have seen his share of human suffering. Nevertheless, his division performed admirably: the 91st captured more artillery, machine guns, and prisoners, and advanced farther under fire than other divisions with more combat experience. Their successes at the Argonne Forest formed a vital part of the "Grand Offensive" by the Allies along the Western Front, regarded as the battle that crushed German hopes for victory and produced the Armistice on November 11, 1918.

For service in the American Expeditionary Force, and love for his adopted country, my grandfather was made a proud citizen of the United States, naturalized on September 15, 1919. He eventually moved to Brooklyn, New York, where he raised his family and helped to launch Conte Farms, an egg-and-dairy delivery business.

Michael and Theodora Loconte are buried in Long Island National Cemetery in Farmingdale, New York.

NOTES

Introduction

1. G. J. Meyer, *A World Undone: The Story of the Great War, 1914–1918* (New York: Random House, 2006), 220.

2. Ibid.

3. "Carols, Plum Pudding, Beer and Bullets," in *The First World War: An Illustrated History, Special 100th Anniversary Commemoration*, 27.

4. Modris Eksteins, *Rites of Spring: The Great War and the Birth of the Modern Age* (New York: Houghton Mifflin, 2000), 110–111.

5. John Keegan, *The First World War* (New York: Alfred A. Knopf, 1999), 8.

6. Paul Johnson, *A History of the American People* (New York: HarperCollins, 1997), 642.

7. Winston Churchill, *The World Crisis, 1911–1918* (New York: Free Press, 2005), 291.

8. Richard Overy, *The Twilight Years: The Paradox of Britain Between the Wars* (London: Penguin, 2009), 363.

9. Gary Sheffield, *Forgotten Victory: The First World War: Myths and Realities* (London: Headline, 2002), xvii.

10. Eksteins, *Rites of Spring*, 237.

11. Roger Sale, *Modern Heroism: Essays on D. H. Lawrence, William Empson, and J. R. R. Tolkien* (Berkeley: University of California Press, 1973), 3.

12. Churchill, *The World Crisis*, 293.

13. Max Hastings, *Catastrophe 1914: Europe Goes to War* (New York: Alfred A. Knopf, 2013), 548.

14. J. R. R. Tolkien, foreword to *The Lord of the Rings* (Boston: Houghton Mifflin, 2004), xxiv.

15. Walter Hooper, ed., *The Collected Letters of C. S. Lewis,* Vol. 2 (New York: HarperSanFrancisco, 2004), 258.

16. K. J. Gilchrist, *A Morning After War: C. S. Lewis and WWI* (New York: Peter Lang, 2005), 218.

17. The phrase appears in Tolkien's essay "On Translating Beowulf" in Christopher Tolkien, ed., *J. R. R. Tolkien: The Monsters and the Critics and Other Essays* (HarperCollins, 2006), 60.

18. Walter Lippman, *A Preface to Morals* (New York: Time-Life Books, 1961), 16.

19. Lee D. Rossi, *The Politics of Fantasy: C. S. Lewis and J. R. R. Tolkien* (Ann Arbor: UMI Research Press, 1984), 4.

20. Patricia Meyer Spacks, "Power and Meaning in *The Lord of the Rings,*" in Rose A. Zimbardo and Neil D. Isaacs, eds., *Understanding The Lord of the Rings: The Best of Tolkien Criticism* (Boston: Houghton Mifflin, 2004), 54.

21. Carol Zaleski, "C. S. Lewis's *Aeneid,*" *The Christian Century,* June 2, 2011. Walter Hooper has written that "Lewis probably read the *Aeneid* more often than he did any other book." Walter Hooper, ed., *The Collected Letters of C. S. Lewis,* Vol. 3 (New York: HarperCollins, 2007), 39.

22. C. S. Lewis, *The Chronicles of Narnia* (New York: HarperCollins, 2001), 147.

23. Walter Hooper, ed., C. S. Lewis, *The Weight of Glory and Other Addresses* (New York: Touchstone, 1996), 51–52.

24. Humphrey Carpenter, *J. R. R. Tolkien: A Biography* (Boston: Houghton Mifflin, 1987), 89.

25. Victor Davis Hanson, *The Father of Us All: War and History* (New York: Bloomsbury Press, 2010), 4.

26. Tolkien, *The Lord of the Rings,* 766.

27. Rossi, *The Politics of Fantasy,* 85, 134.

28. Walter Hooper, ed., *Present Concerns: Essays by C. S. Lewis* (New York: Harcourt Jovanovich, 1986), 42.

29. Humphrey Carpenter, ed., *The Letters of J. R. R. Tolkien* (Boston: Houghton Mifflin, 2000), 75.

30. Tolkien once admitted that "as far as any character is 'like me' it is Faramir—except that I lack what all my characters possess (let the psychoanalysts note!) *Courage.*" Carpenter, ed., *The Letters,* 232.

31. Tolkien, *The Lord of the Rings,* 672.

Chapter 1: The Funeral of a Great Myth

1. Martin Gilbert, *The First World War: A Complete History* (New York: Henry Holt and Company, 1994), 3.
2. Giovanni Pico della Mirandola, *Oration on the Dignity of Man* (Washington DC: Regnery, 1999), 7–8.
3. Hastings, *Catastrophe 1914*, 3.
4. Gilbert, *The First World War: A Complete History*, 3.
5. Norman Angell, *The Great Illusion: A Study of the Relation of Military Power to National Advantage* (Memphis: Bottom of the Hill, 2012), 103.
6. Ibid., 119–120.
7. H. G. Wells, *The New World Order* (London: Secker and Warburg, 1940), 10.
8. Albert Marrin, *The Last Crusade: The Church of England in the First World War* (Durham, NC: Duke University Press, 1974), 66.
9. Niall Ferguson, *Empire: The Rise and Demise of the British World Order and the Lessons for Global Power* (New York: Perseus, 2002), 240.
10. Ibid., xxiv.
11. "Crystal Palace to Rise from the Ashes as Chinese Cash Rebuilds Symbol of Empire," *The Times of London*, Oct. 4, 2013.
12. Roger Osborne, *Civilization: A New History of the Western World* (New York: Pegasus Books, 2006), 400, 420.
13. J. R. R. Tolkien, *Tree and Leaf* (London: HarperCollins, 1988), 63.
14. Carpenter, *J. R. R. Tolkien*, 179.
15. Carpenter, ed., *The Letters*, 250.
16. Ibid., 288.
17. J. R. R. Tolkien, *The Silmarillion*, ed. Christopher Tolkien (Boston: Houghton Mifflin, 1999), xiii. Also in Carpenter, ed., *The Letters*, 146.
18. Carpenter, ed., *The Letters*, 87–88.
19. Tolkien, *The Lord of the Rings*, 473.
20. C. S. Lewis, *Surprised by Joy: The Shape of My Early Life* (San Diego: Harcourt Brace Jovanovich, 1984), 11.
21. Roger Green and Walter Hooper, *C. S. Lewis: A Biography* (New York: Harcourt Brace Jovanovich, 1974), 20.
22. Hooper, ed., *Collected Letters*, Vol. 3, 1480.
23. Lewis, *The Chronicles of Narnia*, 450.
24. Tolkien, *The Lord of the Rings*, 499–500.
25. Alister McGrath, *C. S. Lewis: A Life* (Carol Stream, IL: Tyndale House, 2013), 276.
26. Lewis, *The Chronicles of Narnia*, 353.
27. Ibid., 406.

28. Martin Gilbert, *The Somme: Heroism and Horror in the First World War* (New York: Henry Holt and Company, 2006), 66.
29. Gilbert, *The First World War*, 533.
30. Hastings, *Catastrophe 1914*, 2.
31. Richard Tarnas, *The Passion of the Western Mind* (New York: Ballantine Books, 1991), 319.
32. Osborne, *Civilization*, 400–401.
33. Herbert Spencer, *The Evanescence of Evil* Part I, Chapter 2, concluding paragraph.
34. Richard Hofstadter, *Social Darwinism in American Thought* (Boston: Beacon Press, 1992), 33.
35. Ibid., 35.
36. Ibid., 32.
37. Lesley Walmsley, ed., *C. S. Lewis Essay Collection: Faith, Christianity and the Church* (London: HarperCollins, 2000), 29.
38. Ibid., 26, 28.
39. James Turner, *Without God, Without Creed: The Origins of Unbelief in America* (Baltimore: The Johns Hopkins University Press, 1985), 201.
40. Richard M. Gamble, *The War for Righteousness: Progressive Christianity, the Great War, and the Rise of the Messianic Nation* (Wilmington, DE: ISI Books, 2003), 37.
41. Christine Rosen, *Preaching Eugenics: Religious Leaders and the American Eugenics Movement* (Oxford: Oxford University Press, 2004), 25.
42. Francis Galton, "Eugenics as a Factor in Religion," in *Essays in Eugenics* (London: Eugenics Education Society, 1909). Cited in Rosen, *Preaching Eugenics*, 5.
43. Philipp Blom, *The Vertigo Years: Europe, 1900–1914* (New York: Basic Books, 2008), 339.
44. Rosen, *Preaching Eugenics*, 3–23.
45. Francis Galton, "Eugenics: Its Definition, Scope and Aims," *American Journal of Sociology* 10 (July 1904): 5. Cited in Rosen, *Preaching Eugenics*, 5.
46. Ibid., 33–34.
47. Ibid., 99.
48. Michael D. C. Drout, ed., *J. R. R. Tolkien Encyclopedia* (New York: Routledge, 2007), 555.
49. Carpenter, ed., *The Letters*, 190.
50. Tolkien, *The Lord of the Rings*, 49.

51. C. S. Lewis, *Perelandra* (New York: Macmillan Publishing, 1965), 91.
52. Tolkien, *Tree and Leaf*, 89.
53. C. S. Lewis, *The Abolition of Man* (New York: Touchstone, 1996), 69–70.
54. Hofstadter, *Social Darwinism*, 162.
55. Sermon by Rev. Kenneth C. MacArthur, Federated Church (Congregational Baptist), Sterling, Massachusetts, 1926, AES Papers, APS. Quoted in Rosen, *Preaching Eugenics*, 125.
56. Rosen, *Preaching Eugenics*, 150.
57. Ibid., 184.
58. Ibid.
59. Lewis, *The Chronicles of Narnia*, 416.
60. Carpenter, ed., *The Letters*, 147.
61. Tolkien, *TheLord of the Rings*, 232.
62. Lewis, *The Chronicles of Narnia*, 41.
63. Niall Ferguson, *The War of the World: Twentieth-Century Conflict and the Descent of the West* (New York: Penguin, 2007), 107–108.
64. Ibid., 117.
65. Keegan, *The First World War*, 27, 73.
66. Gilbert, *The First World War*, 29.
67. Ferguson, *The War of the World*, 117.
68. W. M. Spellman, *A Short History of Western Political Thought* (New York: Palgrave Macmillan, 2011), 139.
69. Gamble, *The War for Righteousness*, 32.
70. Osborne, *Civilization*, 368.
71. James Cronan, "The Lamps Are Going Out All Over Europe," The National Archives Blog, August 4, 2014, http://blog.nationalarchives.gov.uk/blog/lamps-going-europe/.

Chapter 2: The Last Battle

1. C. V. Wedgwood, *The Thirty Years War* (New York: Book of the Month Club, 1995), 526.
2. Peter Wilson, *The Thirty Years War: Europe's Tragedy* (London: Penguin, 2009), 5.
3. Wedgwood, *The Thirty Years War*, 526.
4. Wilson, *The Thirty Years War: Europe's Tragedy*, 753.
5. Philip Jenkins, *The Great and Holy War: How World War I Became a Religious Crusade* (New York: HarperOne, 2014), 87–88.
6. Albert Marrin, *The Last Crusade: The Church of England in the First World War* (Durham, North Carolina: Duke University Press, 1974), 139.

7. Queen Victoria reigned in England until her death in 1901. Her eldest son, Edward VII, assumed the throne in 1901 and ruled until his death in 1910. Regarding the values defining family, faith, and the social and political order, "the Edwardians were extensions of the Victorians." Eksteins, *Rites of Spring*, 130.

8. John Garth, *Tolkien and the Great War: The Threshold of Middle-earth* (Boston: Houghton Mifflin, 2003), 20–21.

9. Richard Schweitzer, *The Cross and the Trenches: Religious Faith and Doubt among British and American Great War Soldiers* (Westport, CT: Praeger, 2003), 4.

10. Hooper, ed., *Collected Letters*, Vol. 1, 50.

11. George Sayer, *Jack: A Life of C. S. Lewis* (Wheaton, IL: Crossway, 1994), 77.

12. Hooper, ed., *Collected Letters*, Vol. 1, 71.

13. Carpenter, ed., *The Letters*, 232.

14. Garth, *Tolkien and the Great War*, 43.

15. Carpenter, *J.R. R. Tolkien*, 91.

16. Don W. King, *C. S. Lewis: The Legacy of His Poetic Impulse* (Kent, OH: Kent State University Press, 2001), 55.

17. Hooper, ed., *Collected Letters*, Vol. 1, 89.

18. Ibid., 88.

19. Ferguson, *Empire*, 359.

20. Eksteins, *Rites of Spring*, 179.

21. John Ellis, *Eye-Deep in Hell: Trench Warfare in World War I* (Baltimore: The Johns Hopkins University Press, 1976), 162.

22. Eksteins, *Rites of Spring*, 179–180.

23. http://www.firstworldwar.com/source/asquithspeechtoparliament.htm.

24. Eksteins, *Rites of Spring*, 236.

25. Michael Burleigh, *Earthly Powers: Religion and Politics in Europe from the French Revolution to the Great War* (London: HarperCollins, 2005), 144–145.

26. Quoted in Marrin, *The Last Crusade*, 59.

27. Alasdair I. C. Heron, *A Century of Protestant Theology* (Philadelphia: The Westminster Press, 1980), 75.

28. Joseph Fort Newton, *The Sword of the Spirit: Britain and America in the Great War* (New York: George H. Coran), xiii, xv.

29. John Spurr, *The Post-Reformation: 1603–1714* (Harlow, England: Pearson Longman, 2006), 16.

30. A. J. Hoover, *God, Germany, and Britain in the Great War: A Study in Clerical Nationalism* (New York: Praeger, 1989), 69.

31. Ibid.

32. Stuart Mews, "Spiritual Mobilization in the First World War," *Theology* (1971), 74:258, 259.

33. Hoover, *God, Germany, and Britain in the Great War*, 69.

34. Marrin, *The Last Crusade*, 177–186.

35. Conrad Cherry, ed., *God's New Israel: Religious Interpretations of American Destiny* (Chapel Hill: The University of North Carolina Press, 1998), 83.

36. Ibid., 64–65.

37. Woodrow Wilson, "Address to Congress Requesting a Declaration of War Against Germany (April 2, 1917), University of Virginia Miller Center, http://millercenter.org/president/wilson/speeches/speech-4722.

38. Cherry, ed., *God's New Israel*, 276.

39. Andrew Preston, *Sword of the Spirit, Shield of Faith* (New York: Alfred A. Knopf, 2012), 254.

40. Ray H. Abrams, *Preachers Present Arms: The Role of American Churches and Clergy in World War I and II with Some Observations on the War in Vietnam* (Eugene, Oregon: Wipf & Stock, 1969), 55.

41. Burleigh, *Earthly Powers*, 444.

42. Hoover, *God, Germany, and Britain in the Great War*, 94.

43. Ernst Troeltsch, *Deutscher Glaube und deutsche Sitte in unserem grossen Kriege* (Berlin: n.d.), 19. Cited in Burleigh, *Earthly Powers*, 442.

44. Ibid., 442.

45. The Allied nations accused the Kaiser and the German people of blasphemy because of their confident intimacy with God, expressed in phrases such as *Gott mit uns*, a phrase later picked up by the Nazis.

46. Jenkins, *The Great and Holy War*, 12.

47. Hoover, *God, Germany, and Britain in the Great War*, 2. Hubbard perished aboard the RMS *Lusitania*, which was sunk by a German submarine off the coast of Ireland on May 7, 1915.

48. Hooper, ed., *Collected Letters*, Vol. 1, 83.

49. Dan Todman, *The Great War: Myth and Memory* (London: Bloomsbury, 2005), 124.

50. *First World War: An Illustrated History*, 44.

51. Meyer, *A World Undone*, 297.

52. Hoover, *God, Germany, and Britain in the Great War*, 24.

53. Ibid., 29.

54. Ibid., 24.

55. Marrin, *The Last Crusade*, 137–138.

56. Abrams, *Preachers Present Arms*, 104.

57. Ibid., 108.

58. Ibid., 104.

59. Hoover, *God, Germany, and Britain in the Great War*, 9.

60. Gamble, *The War for Righteousness*, 160.

61. Basil Mathews, ed., *Christ: And the World at War* (London: James Clarke & Co., 1917), 46.

62. Ibid., 170.

63. Gamble, *The War for Righteousness*, 3.

64. Preston, *Sword of the Spirit, Shield of Faith*, 275.

65. Joseph Fort Newton, *The Sword of the Spirit: Britain and America in the Great War* (New York: George H. Doran, 1918), 38.

66. Gamble, *The War for Righteousness*, 175.

67. Paul Bull, *Christianity and War*, quoted in Kevin Christopher Fielden, "The Church of England in the First World War" (Electronic Theses and Dissertations. Paper 1080, 2005), http://dc.etsu.edu/etd/1080.

68. C. S. Lewis, *The Weight of Glory* (New York: HarperCollins, 2001), 51.

69. Although there have been some excellent studies of the religious faith of soldiers during the war years, we should be careful not to generalize too much about their personal beliefs or their views of the ultimate meaning of the conflict. See Rich Schweitzer, *The Cross and the Trenches: Religious Faith and Doubt Among British and American Great War Soldiers* (Santa Barbara, CA: Praeger, 2003).

70. Ellis, *Eye-Deep in Hell*, 156.

71. Schweitzer, *The Cross and the Trenches*, 168.

72. Burleigh, *Earthly Powers*, 451.

73. Robert Graves, *Good-Bye to All That* (New York: Vintage International, 1998), 189.

74. Marrin, *The Last Crusade*, 242–243.

75. Graves, *Good-Bye to All That*, 189.

76. Schweitzer, *The Cross and the Trenches*, 259.

77. Burleigh, *Earthly Powers*, 453.

78. Schweitzer, *The Cross and the Trenches*, 81–82.

79. Keegan, *The First World War*, 289.

80. Jonathan Phillips, *Holy Warrior: A Modern History of the Crusades* (New York: Random House, 2010), 323.

81. Tolkien, *The Lord of the Rings*, 243.

82. Carpenter, ed., *The Letters*, 197.

83. Lewis, *The Chronicles of Narnia*, 455.

84. C. S. Lewis, *That Hideous Strength* (New York: Simon & Schuster, 1996), 178.

85. Tolkien, *The Lord of the Rings*, 60.
86. Lewis, *The Chronicles of Narnia*, 170.
87. Lewis, *The Weight of Glory*, 70.
88. Tolkien, *The Lord of the Rings*, 140.

Chapter 3: In a Hole in the Ground There Lived a Hobbit

1. "The Battle of Jutland, 1916," Eye Witness to History, 2006, http://www.eyewitnesstohistory.com/pfjutland.htm.
2. Gilbert, *The First World War*, 252.
3. Garth, *Tolkien and the Great War*, 58–59.
4. Meyer, *A World Undone*, 361.
5. "The Battle of Verdun," History Learning Site, 2014, http://www.historylearningsite.co.uk/battle_of_verdun.htm.
6. Charles F. Horne, ed., *Source Records of the Great War*, Vol. IV (National Alumni, 1923), http://www.firstworldwar.com/diaries/verdun_vaux.htm.
7. Meyer, *A World Undone*, 427.
8. Alistair Horne, *The Price of Glory* (London: Macmillan, 1962), 236.
9. Garth, *Tolkien and the Great War*, 138.
10. The precise date of Tolkien's Channel crossing with his battalion was June 6, 1916.
11. Tolkien, "The Lonely Isle," http://webpages.charter.net/sn9/literature/poetry/2tolkienpoems.html.
12. Tolkien, *The Lord of the Rings*, 62.
13. Eksteins, *Rites of Spring*, 178.
14. Keegan, *The Face of Battle*, 221.
15. Garth, *Tolkien and the Great War*, 41.
16. Carpenter, ed., *The Letters*, 53.
17. Keegan, *The Face of Battle*, 221.
18. Mathews, *Christ: And the World at War*, 134–35.
19. Carpenter, ed., *The Letters*, 53.
20. Meyer, *A World Undone*, 363.
21. Eksteins, *Rites of Spring*, 180.
22. Garth, *Tolkien and the Great War*, 188.
23. Paul Fussell, *The Great War and Modern Memory* (Oxford: Oxford University Press, 2013), 51.
24. Ibid., 52.
25. Keegan, *The First World War*, 52.
26. Hastings, *Catastrophe 1914*, 516.
27. Gilbert, *The Somme*, 194.
28. Carpenter, ed., *The Letters*, 231.

29. Tolkien, *The Lord of the Rings*, 822.
30. Gilbert, *The Somme*, 71.
31. Keegan, *The Face of Battle*, 260.
32. Meyer, *A World Undone*, 446.
33. David Lloyd George, *War Memoirs of David Lloyd George, 1915–1916* (Boston: Little Brown, 1933).
34. Gilbert, *The Somme*, 269.
35. Keegan, *The First World War*, 295.
36. Churchill, *The World Crisis*, 667.
37. Gilbert, *The Somme*, 64.
38. Sir Martin Gilbert, "What Tolkien Taught Me About the Battle of the Somme," *The Cutting Edge*, August 25, 2008, http://www.thecuttingedgenews.com/index.php?article=716&pageid=23&pagename=Arts.
39. Garth, *Tolkien and the Great War*, 155.
40. Tolkien, *The Lord of the Rings*, 6.
41. Garth, *Tolkien and the Great War*, 157.
42. Keegan, *The Face of Battle*, 231.
43. G. J. Meyer, *A World Undone*, 261.
44. Tolkien, *The Lord of the Rings*, 765, italics added.
45. Ibid., 188.
46. Carpenter, ed., *The Letters*, 221.
47. Ibid. The italics are mine.
48. Garth, *Tolkien and the Great War*, 161.
49. Ibid., 114.
50. Ibid., 164.
51. Ibid., 166.
52. Keegan, *The First World War*, 296.
53. Philip Gibbs, *The Battles of the Somme* (Toronto: McClelland, Goodchild, and Stewart, 1917), 6.
54. Garth, *Tolkien and the Great War*, 165–166.
55. Ibid., 166.
56. Carpenter, ed., *The Letters*, 72.
57. Carpenter, *J. R. R. Tolkien*, 92.
58. Gilbert, *The Somme*, 140–141.
59. Carpenter, ed., *The Letters*, 9.
60. Tolkien, *The Lord of the Rings*, 883.
61. Garth, *Tolkien and the Great War*, 193.
62. Ellis, *Eye-Deep in Hell*, 96.
63. Tolkien, *The Lord of the Rings*, 808.

64. Ellis, *Eye-Deep in Hell*, 98.
65. Gilbert, *The Somme*, 85.
66. Ibid., 220.
67. Carpenter, *J. R. R. Tolkien*, 94.
68. Tolkien, ed., *The Monsters and the Critics*, 60.
69. Carpenter, *J. R. R. Tolkien*, 91.
70. Tolkien, *The Lord of the Rings*, 828.
71. Nancy Marie Ott, "J. R. R. Tolkien and World War I," at http://greenbooks.theonering.net/guest/files/040102_02.html.
72. Tolkien, *The Lord of the Rings*, 626.
73. Ibid., 631–32.
74. Ibid., 627–28.
75. Gilbert, "What Tolkien Taught Me About the Battle of the Somme."
76. Gilbert, *The Somme*, 239–240.
77. Carpenter, ed., *The Letters*, 303.
78. Ibid., 215. Also in Tom Shippey, *J. R. R. Tolkien: Author of the Century* (Boston: Houghton Mifflin, 2002), 2.
79. Sheffield, *Forgotten Victory*, 157.
80. Ibid.
81. Tolkien, *The Lord of the Rings*, 934.
82. Keegan, *The Face of Battle*, 219.
83. Churchill, *The World Crisis*, 667–668.
84. Gibbs, *The Battles of the Somme*, 18.
85. Carpenter, ed., *The Letters*, 158.
86. Tolkien, *The Lord of the Rings*, 52.

Chapter 4: The Lion, the Witch, and the War

1. Hooper, ed., *Collected Letters*, Vol. 1, 70.
2. Ibid., 72.
3. Ibid., 113.
4. Ibid., 111.
5. Garth, *Tolkien and the Great War*, 42.
6. Homer, *The Iliad*, Introduction and Notes by Bernard Fox (London: Penguin Books, 1998), 26.
7. Gilchrist, *A Morning After War*, 27.
8. Ibid., 26.
9. Hooper, ed., *Collected Letters*, Vol. 1, 125.
10. George MacDonald, *Phantastes* (Grand Rapids: Eerdmans, 1992), xi.
11. George MacDonald, *The Complete Fairy Tales* (Penguin Books, 1999), 9.
12. W. H. Lewis, ed., *Letters of C. S. Lewis* (San Diego: Harcourt, 1988), 179.

13. Ibid., 27.

14. Green and Hooper, *C. S. Lewis: A Biography*, 45.

15. In a letter dated January 21, 1960, Lewis commends MacDonald's works to John Warwick Montgomery. Hooper, ed., *The Letters*, Vol. 3, 1125.

16. Sayer, *Jack*, 107–108.

17. Hooper, ed., *Collected Letters*, Vol. 1, 129.

18. Ibid., 131.

19. Ferguson, *The War of the World*, 127.

20. Douglas Gresham, *Jack's Life: The Life Story of C. S. Lewis* (Nashville: Broadman & Holman, 2005), 33.

21. Hooper, ed., *Collected Letters*, Vol. 1, 171.

22. Ibid., 208–209.

23. Ibid., 204.

24. Ibid., 212.

25. Gilbert, *The Somme*, 71.

26. Hooper, ed., *C. S. Lewis: The Weight of Glory*, 51.

27. Lewis, *Surprised by Joy*, 138.

28. Lewis, ed., *Letters of C. S. Lewis*, 126.

29. Hooper, ed., *Collected Letters*, Vol. 1, 230.

30. Ibid., 230–231.

31. Ibid., 342.

32. Lewis, *Surprised by Joy*, 158.

33. Sayer, *Jack*, 122.

34. Hooper, ed., *Collected Letters*, Vol. 1, 299.

35. Ibid., 310.

36. Lewis, *Surprised by Joy*, 158.

37. Hooper, ed., *Collected Letters*, Vol. 1, 315.

38. Ibid., 319.

39. Ibid., 338.

40. Ibid., 341.

41. Ibid., 346. Walter Hooper placed Lewis at Monchy-Le-Preux, but K. J. Gilchrist disagrees, believing Lewis was in a staging town west of Arras. See Gilchrist, *A Morning After War*, 57–58.

42. Ibid., 351.

43. Gilchrist, *A Morning After War*, 56.

44. Ibid., 63. The descriptions of enemy fire are taken from the diary for Lewis's battalion of the Somerset Light Infantry, known as the "War Diary or Intelligence Summary."

45. Lewis, *Surprised by Joy*, 195.

46. Ibid.
47. C. S. Lewis, *Spirits in Bondage: A Cycle of Lyrics* (Lexington, KY: Emereo, 2013).
48. McGrath, *C. S. Lewis: A Life*, x.
49. Lewis, *Spirits in Bondage*, 9.
50. Fussell, *The Great War and Modern Memory*, 123.
51. Hooper, ed., *Collected Letters*, Vol. 1, 356.
52. Ibid., 363.
53. Gilbert, *The First World War*, 408.
54. From March 21 until May 2, British casualties hit 280,000. The French sustained 340,000 casualties.
55. Walter Hooper, *C .S. Lewis: Companion and Guide* (New York: HarperCollins, 1996), 11.
56. Hooper, ed., *Collected Letters*, Vol. 1, 363.
57. Various biographical references to Lewis's wartime experience incorrectly place him at the 1917 Battle of Arras. In fact, Lewis fought in a different battle, near the village of Arras, in April 1918.
58. Meyer, *A World Undone*, 652.
59. Gilchrist, *A Morning After War*, 123.
60. Lewis, *Surprised by Joy*, 96.
61. Hooper, ed., *Collected Letters*, Vol. 1, 388.
62. Lewis, *Surprised by Joy*, 191.
63. Ibid., 191–192.
64. Ibid., 192.
65. Ibid., 193.
66. Lewis, *Surprised by Joy*, 196.
67. Clyde S. Kilby and Marjorie Lamp Mead, eds., *Brothers and Friends: The Diaries of Major Warren Hamilton Lewis* (New York: Ballantine Books, 1982), 6.
68. Hooper, ed., *Collected Letters*, Vol. 1, 368.
69. Ibid., 414.
70. Sayer, *Jack*, 134.
71. Percy Dearmer, ed., *Christianity and the Crisis* (London: Victor Golancz, 1933), 25–26.
72. Lewis, *That Hideous Strength*, 203–204.
73. Lewis, *Surprised by Joy*, 196.
74. Hooper, ed., *Collected Letters*, Vol. 1, 375.
75. Ibid., 374.
76. MacDonald, *Phantastes*, 149.

Chapter 5: The Land of Shadow

1. Margaret MacMillan, *Paris 1919* (New York: Random House, 2003), 15.
2. Ibid.
3. Churchill, *The World Crisis*, 841.
4. Barbara Tuchman, *The Guns of August* (New York: Ballantine, 1990), 523.
5. Dan Todman offers a nuanced look at what is called "the formation of the modern myth of the war." Views about WWI, he argues, changed over time: "Anyone putting forward in public the idea that the war had been an incompetently run and colossally futile waste of life, unmitigated by any redeeming heroism, would have been chased from the street in the early 1920s." See Todman, *The Great War*, 221–230. Niall Ferguson offers a somewhat contrarian view: "As has often been remarked, the memoirs of the 1920s and 1930s were disproportionately the work of public school and university-educated men with little pre-war experience of hardship, much less war. Their disillusionment was predicated on the illusions of privileged youth." Niall Ferguson, *The Pity of War: Explaining World War 1* (New York: Penguin Press, 1999), 451.
6. David Fromkin, *A Peace to End All Peace: The Fall of the Ottoman Empire and the Creation of the Modern Middle East* (New York: Henry Holt and Company, 1989), 212.
7. It is generally recognized that the Armenian genocide began on April 24, 1915, when the Turkish government arrested and executed several hundred Armenian intellectuals. Soon, Armenians were forced from their homes and men, women, and children were sent on death marches across the Syrian desert to concentration camps. Out of a population of 2 million Armenians living in the Ottoman Empire at the start of the war, an estimated 1.5 million died in the genocide.
8. Eksteins, *Rites of Spring*, 255.
9. Gilbert, *The First World War*, 534.
10. Fussell, *The Great War and Modern Memory*, 342.
11. Erich Maria Remarque, *All Quiet on the Western Front* (New York: Ballantine, 1982), 294.
12. Overy, *The Twilight Years*, 3.
13. Ibid., 15.
14. Oswald Spengler, *The Decline of the West* (New York: Alfred A. Knopf, 1962), 34.
15. Carpenter, ed., *The Letters*, 393.
16. Ibid., 46.
17. Carpenter, *J. R. R. Tolkien*, 108.

18. Ibid., 76.

19. Garth, *Tolkien and the Great War*, 250.

20. Hooper, ed., *Collected Letters*, Vol. 1, 419. After being out of the war for nearly four months because of his injuries, Lewis expected to be sent back into battle; such were the military needs of Great Britain until the day of the Armistice. "Of course in the present need for men, being passed fit by a board would mean a pretty quick return to France," he wrote his father on September 3, 1918. "Although I am not quite well I am almost 'fit' now in the military sense of the word, and depend only on the forgetfulness of the authorities for my continued stay in hospital." Ibid., 395–396.

21. Ibid., 423.

22. Ibid., 428.

23. Lewis, *Letters of C. S. Lewis*, 129.

24. Hooper, ed., *Collected Letters*, Vol. 2, 747.

25. Humphrey Carpenter, *The Inklings: C. S. Lewis, J. R. R. Tolkien, Charles Williams, and Their Friends* (Boston: Houghton Mifflin, 1979), 11.

26. Hooper, ed., *Collected Letters*, Vol. 1, 606.

27. Walter Hooper, ed., *All My Road Before Me: The Diary of C. S. Lewis, 1922–1927* (San Diego: Harcourt, 1991), 135.

28. Susan Kingsley Kent, *The Influenza Pandemic of 1918–1919: A Brief History with Documents* (Boston: Bedford/St. Martin's, 2013), 48.

29. Ibid., 1.

30. Ferguson, *The War of the World*, 144.

31. Kent, *The Influenza Pandemic of 1918–1919*, 2–3.

32. Conversation with Carmella Parrinello, December 28, 2014.

33. Meyer, *A World Undone*, 513.

34. Paul Johnson, *Modern Times: The World from the Twenties to the Nineties* (New York: HarperCollins, 1991), 67.

35. Hooper, ed., *Collected Letters*, Vol. 1, 502.

36. Burleigh, *Sacred Causes*, 58.

37. Michael J. Oakeshott, *The Social and Political Doctrines of Contemporary Europe* (Cambridge: Cambridge University Press, 1939), 164–68.

38. Johnson, *Modern Times*, 103.

39. Gilbert Murray, *The Ordeal of This Generation: The War, the League and the Future* (London: George Allen & Unwin, 1929), 180–181.

40. Eksteins, *Rites of Spring*, 257.

41. Johnson, *Modern Times*, 5.

42. Hooper, ed., *All My Road Before Me*, 212.

43. Hooper, ed., *Collected Letters*, Vol. 1, 605–606.
44. Johnson, *Modern Times*, 5.
45. Sigmund Freud, *The Future of an Illusion* (London: Hogarth Press, 1927), 28.
46. Eksteins, *Rites of Spring*, 256.
47. Dearmer, *Christianity and the Crisis*, 68.
48. Ernest Hemingway, *A Farewell to Arms* (New York: Charles Scribner's Sons, 1969), 185.
49. Walter Hooper, ed., *God in the Dock* (Grand Rapids, MI: Eerdmans, 1970), 116.
50. Garth, *Tolkien and the Great War*, 250.
51. Tolkien, *The Silmarillion*, 242.
52. Ibid., 243.
53. Carpenter, *J. R. R. Tolkien*, 100.
54. Carpenter, ed., *The Letters*, 78.
55. Ibid., 144.
56. Ibid., 231.
57. Tolkien, *The Lord of the Rings*, 836.
58. Niall Ferguson contests the claim that the memory of war in literature and art was one of unqualified horror. "The overwhelming majority of the vast number of poems written during the war by combatants and non-combatants alike were patriotic ditties." Ferguson, *The Pity of War*, 48–49.
59. Candace Ward, ed., *World War One British Poets* (Mineola, NY: Dover Publications, 1997), 25.
60. Ibid., 36.
61. Todman, *The Great War*, 155.
62. Graves, *Goodbye to All That*, 186.
63. Carpenter, ed., *The Letters*, 75–76.
64. Walter Hooper, ed., *C. S. Lewis: Of This and Other Worlds* (London: Fount, 2000), 100–101.
65. Shippey, *J. R. R. Tolkien: Author of the Century*, 232.
66. Tolkien, *The Silmarillion*, xv.
67. Carpenter, ed., *The Letters*, 203.
68. Ibid., 239.
69. This was Lewis's first article published outside of college publications.
70. Hooper, ed., *Collected Letters*, Vol. 1, 397.
71. Lewis, *Spirits in Bondage*, 7.
72. Fussell, *The Great War and Modern Memory*, 364.
73. Churchill, *The World Crisis*, 4.

74. Jenkins, *The Great and Holy War*, 223.
75. The Bloomsbury Group was an influential association of English writers, intellectuals, philosophers, and artists, which included Virginia Woolf, John Maynard Keynes, E. M. Forster, and Lytton Strachey. They lived and collaborated together near Bloomsbury, London, during the first half of the twentieth century.
76. Hooper, *C. S. Lewis: Companion and Guide*, 25.
77. Murray, *The Ordeal of This Generation*, 173.
78. Friedrich Nietzsche, *Beyond Good and Evil* (New York: Penguin, 1990), 82.
79. Hooper, ed., *All My Road BeforeMe*, 431–432.
80. Sayer, *Jack*, 219.
81. Lewis, *Surprised by Joy*, 199–200.
82. C. S. Lewis, *The Pilgrim's Regress* (Grand Rapids, MI: Eerdmans, 1992), 205.
83. Hooper, ed., *Collected Letters*, Vol. 1, 509.
84. Ibid., 649.
85. Ibid.
86. Ibid., 850.
87. In a letter to Arthur Greeves dated March 25, 1933, Lewis mentioned a talk with Tolkien "who, you know, grew up on Morris and Macdonald and shares my taste in literature to a fault." Hooper, ed., *The Letters*, Vol. 2, 103.
88. Hooper, ed., *Collected Letters*, Vol. 1, 918.
89. There is no written record of their precise conversation, but Carpenter does an admirable job of reconstructing their talk, based on Tolkien's poem "Mythopoeia." I have followed Carpenter's narrative and added to it based on Tolkien's and Lewis's other letters and writings. See Carpenter, *J.R.R. Tolkien: A Biography*, 150–152.
90. Ibid., 234–235.
91. Carpenter, *The Inklings*, 43.
92. Carpenter, ed., *The Letters*, 110–111.
93. Carpenter, *J.R.R. Tolkien*, 151.
94. Tolkien, *Tree and Leaf*, 87.
95. Carpenter, *The Inklings*, 44. See also Lewis's letter to Arthur Greeves in Hooper, ed., *Collected Letters*, Vol. 1, 976.
96. Carpenter, *J.R.R. Tolkien*, 151.
97. Tolkien, *Tree and Leaf*, 90.
98. Carpenter, *J. R. R. Tolkien*, 151.
99. Lewis, *Surprised by Joy*, 136.

100. Hooper, ed., *Collected Letters*, 974.
101. The first book that Lewis wrote after his conversion to Christianity, *The Pilgrim's Regress,* traces his own intellectual and spiritual search for truth.
102. Lewis, *Surprised by Joy*, 225.
103. Hooper, ed., *C. S. Lewis: Of This and Other Worlds*, 7.
104. Hooper, ed., *Collected Letters*, Vol. 2, 501.
105. Carpenter, ed., *The Letters*, 388.
106. Ibid., 29.
107. Ibid., 341.
108. Hooper, ed., *Collected Letters*, Vol. 2, 262.
109. Carpenter, ed., *The Letters*, 209.
110. Ibid.
111. J. R. R. Tolkien, *The Hobbit* (New York: Ballantine, 1973), 17.
112. Carpenter, *J. R. R. Tolkien: A Biography*, 180.
113. Tolkien, *The Hobbit*, 268.
114. Hooper, ed., *Collected Letters*, Vol. 2, 631.
115. Carpenter, ed., *The Letters*, 388.
116. Ibid., 68.
117. Hooper, ed. *Collected Letters*, Vol. 2, 990.
118. Carpenter, ed., *The Letters*, 362.
119. John Bunyan, *The Pilgrim's Progress* (London: Penguin, 2008), 67.
120. Philip Gibbs, *Now It Can Be Told* (New York: Harper and Brothers, 1920), 131.
121. Tolkien, *The Lord of the Rings*, 518.
122. Ibid., 61.
123. Lewis, *The Chronicles of Narnia*, 81.

Chapter 6: *That Hideous Strength*

1. Thucydides, *The Peloponnesian War* (Oxford: Oxford University Press, 2009), 98.
2. Ibid., 99.
3. Meyer, *A World Undone*, 396.
4. Ibid., 397.
5. Hooper, ed., *C. S. Lewis: Of This and Other Worlds*, 95.
6. Ibid., 98.
7. Ibid., 102.
8. See Tom Shippey, *J. R. R. Tolkien: Author of the Century* (Boston: Houghton Mifflin, 2000), xvii–xxxv.

9. Roger Sale, "Tolkien and Frodo Baggins," in Neil D. Isaacs and Rose A. Zimbardo, eds., *Tolkien and the Critics: Essays on J. R. R. Tolkien's* The Lord of the Rings (Notre Dame: University of Notre Dame Press, 1972), 247.

10. Ernst Jünger, *Storm of Steel* (New York: Penguin, 2004), 71.

11. Meyer, *A World Undone*, 547.

12. In a letter to Jocelyn Gibb, dated April 16, 1961, Lewis is bemused by the author David Richard Davies, who seemed to discover, because of the Spanish Civil War, that humanity was capable of great wickedness. Wrote Lewis: "Most of us learned this during the First German War." Hooper, ed., *Collected Letters*, Vol. 3, 1254–1255.

13. This is Lyndsay's description of the biblical Tower of Babel. Lewis borrowed the line for the title of the third book in his science fiction series, *That Hideous Strength*.

14. Tolkien, *The Lord of the Rings*, 47.

15. Ibid., 267.

16. Shippey, *J. R. R. Tolkien: Author of the Century*, 114. I am indebted to Shippey's excellent treatment of this theme. See 112–160.

17. Ibid., 630.

18. C. S. Lewis, *The Screwtape Letters* (New York: MacMillan, 1982), x.

19. Lewis, *The Chronicles of Narnia*, 47.

20. Ibid., 118.

21. Ibid., 62.

22. See Carpenter, ed., *The Letters*, 173.

23. Carpenter, ed., *The Letters*, 76.

24. Lewis, *That Hideous Strength*, 293.

25. Hooper, *C. S. Lewis: Companion and Guide*, 240.

26. See Shippey, *J. R. R. Tolkien: Author of the Century*, 112–160.

27. Tolkien, *The Lord of the Rings*, 51.

28. Ibid., 268–269.

29. Ibid., 331.

30. Tolkien, *The Silmarillion*, 298.

31. Tolkien, *The Lord of the Rings*, 357.

32. Ibid., 358.

33. Hooper, ed., *C. S. Lewis: Of This and Other Worlds*, 28.

34. Tolkien, *The Lord of the Rings*, 777.

35. Lewis, *The Chronicles of Narnia*, 82.

36. Carpenter, ed., *The Letters*, 172.

37. Tolkien, *The Lord of the Rings*, 61.

38. Lewis, *The Chronicles of Narnia*, 271.

39. Tolkien, *The Lord of the Rings*, 199.

40. Ibid., 222.

41. Drout, *J. R. R. Tolkien Encyclopedia*, 75.

42. Tolkien, *The Lord of the Rings*, 398.

43. Ibid., 259.

44. Lewis, *The Chronicles of Narnia*, 393.

45. Lewis, *That Hideous Strength*, 203.

46. Ibid.

47. Shippey, *J. R. R. Tolkien: Author of the Century*, 117.

48. Tolkien, *The Lord of the Rings*, 267.

49. Ibid., 269.

50. Carpenter, ed., *The Letters*, 246.

51. Isaacs and Zimbardo, eds., *Tolkien and the Critics*, 36.

52. C. S. Lewis put it this way: "These things were not devised to reflect any particular situation in the real world. It was the other way around; real events began, horribly, to conform to the pattern he had freely invented." See Carpenter, *Tolkien: A Biography*, 193.

53. Carpenter, ed., *The Letters*, 332.

54. Tolkien, *The Lord of the Rings*, 945.

55. Lewis, *The Screwtape Letters*, 56.

56. Lewis, *That Hideous Strength*, 130.

57. Lewis, *The Chronicles of Narnia*, 125–126.

58. Arthur Weinberg, ed., *Attorney for the Damned: Clarence Darrow in the Courtroom* (Chicago: University of Chicago Press, 2012), 56.

59. Johnson, *Modern Times*, 71.

60. Ibid., 70.

61. Lewis, *The Chronicles of Narnia*, 258.

62. Genesis 4:7.

63. Tolkien once received a letter from an admirer, a self-described "unbeliever" who nonetheless found himself drawn to the religious sensibility of the story. "You create a world in which some sort of faith seems to be everywhere without a visible source, like light from an invisible lamp." Carpenter, ed., *The Letters*, 413.

64. Hooper, ed., *C. S. Lewis: Of This and Other Worlds*, 99.

65. Ferguson, *The Pity of War*, 186.

66. Thomas Hardy, *The Collected Poems of Thomas Hardy* (Ware, Hertfordshire: Wordsworth Editions, 1994), 509.

67. Tolkien, *The Lord of the Rings*, 531.

68. Croft, *War and the Works of J. R. R. Tolkien*, 16–17.

69. Tolkien, *The Lord of the Rings*, 849.

70. Ibid., 848.

71. Ibid., 631–632.

72. Ibid., 458.

73. Ibid., 823.

74. Croft, *War and the Works of J. R. R. Tolkien*, 26.

75. Brian Rosebury, *Tolkien: A Critical Assessment* (New York: St. Martin's, 1992), 126.

76. Lewis, *The Chronicles of Narnia*, 292.

77. Ibid., 170–171.

78. Brian Melton, "The Great War and Narnia: C. S. Lewis as Soldier and Creator," *Mythlore*, September 22, 2011. Much of my analysis follows closely that of Melton's fine treatment of this theme.

79. Lewis, *The Chronicles of Narnia*, 358.

80. Ibid., 732.

81. In an essay exploring his groundbreaking translation of *Beowulf*, for example, Tolkien explained that the men of these legends "were conceived as kings of chivalrous courts" and that "the imagination of the author of *Beowulf* moved upon the threshold of Christian chivalry, if indeed it had not already passed within." Tolkien, ed., *The Monsters and the Critics*, 57.

82. Garth, *Tolkien and the Great War*, 292.

83. Lewis, *The Chronicles of Narnia*, 650.

84. Ibid., 402.

85. I am indebted to Verlyn Flieger's analysis of the heroic tradition in *The Lord of the Rings* in her essay, "Frodo and Aragorn: The Concept of the Hero," in Zimbardo and Isaacs, eds., *Understanding The Lord of the Rings*, 122–125.

86. Zimbardo and Isaacs, eds., *Understanding The Lord of the Rings*, 123.

87. Tolkien, *The Lord of the Rings*, 171.

88. Ibid., 62.

89. Eksteins, *Rites of Spring*, 258.

90. Hooper, ed., *Present Concerns*, 15.

91. Lee Rossi, *The Politics of Fantasy: C. S. Lewis and J. R. R. Tolkien* (Ann Arbor: UMI Research Press, 1984), 2.

92. As Lewis put it in *The Discarded Image*: "I hope no one will think I am recommending a return to the Medieval Model. I am only suggesting considerations that may induce us to regard all Models in the right way, respecting each and idolizing none." C. S. Lewis, *The Discarded Image: An Introduction to Medieval and Renaissance Literature* (Cambridge: Cambridge University, 2003), 222.

93. Hooper, ed., *Present Concerns*, 14.
94. Carpenter, ed., *The Letters*, 160.
95. Ibid., 179.
96. Hooper, ed., *Present Concerns*, 16.
97. Stephen E. Ambrose, *Band of Brothers* (New York: Simon and Schuster, 1992), 61.
98. Alan Jacobs, *The Narnian: The Life and Imagination of C. S. Lewis* (New York: HarperOne, 2006), 88.
99. Lewis, *The Chronicles of Narnia*, 583.
100. Ibid., 244.
101. See Mike Bellah, *A Celebration of Joy: Christian Romanticism in the Chronicles of Narnia*, http://www.bestyears.com/thesis__7.html.
102. C. S. Lewis, *The Four Loves* (San Diego: Harcourt Brace Jovanovich, 1988), 87. See Lewis's excellent treatment of the theme of friendship in this work, 87–127.
103. Kilby and Mead, eds., *Brothers and Friends*, 284.
104. Lewis, *The Four Loves*, 104.
105. Alister McGrath convincingly argued that Lewis joined the Somerset Light Infantry so that he could serve alongside his friend Paddy Moore. See McGrath, *C. S. Lewis*, 65–66.
106. Tolkien, *The Lord of the Rings*, 105.
107. Ibid., 104.
108. Carpenter, ed., *The Letters*, 88.
109. Tolkien, *The Lord of the Rings*, 87.
110. Ibid., 940.
111. Members of the Inklings included Lewis and his brother Warren, Tolkien, Charles Williams, Owen Barfield, and Hugo Dyson.
112. Carpenter, ed., *The Letters*, 94.
113. Hooper, ed., *Collected Letters*, Vol. 2, 501.
114. Carpenter, ed., *The Letters*, 303.
115. Hooper, ed., *Collected Letters*, Vol. 3, 249–250.
116. In his letter to Tolkien, dated November 13, 1952, Lewis does not explicitly refer to the First World War in his mention of "the war" as among the things that Tolkien's work had helped to make permanent. But it seems unlikely that he would have the Second World War in mind, which had come to an end seven years earlier.
117. Hooper, ed., *Collected Letters*, Vol. 3, 1458.
118. Tolkien, *The Lord of the Rings*, 694. Italics are mine.
119. Carpenter, ed., *The Letters*, 341.

120. Lewis, *The Chronicles of Narnia*, 216.
121. Tolkien, *The Lord of the Rings*, 870.
122. Ibid., 500.
123. Spacks, "Power and Meaning in *The Lord of the Rings*," in Zimbardo and Isaacs, eds., *Understanding The Lord of the Rings*, 60.
124. Ward, ed., *World War One British Poets*, 25.
125. Carpenter, ed., *The Letters*, 78.

Conclusion: The Return of the King

1. "November 11th 1918," History Learning Site, http://www .historylearningsite.co.uk/november_11_1918.htm
2. Thomas Hardy, "And There Was a Great Calm," in Ward, ed., *World War One British Poets*, 58.
3. Meyer, *A World Undone*, 486.
4. Hooper, *C. S. Lewis: Companion and Guide*, 444.
5. Lewis, *The Chronicles of Narnia*, 717.
6. Walmsley, ed., *Faith, Christianity and the Church*, 46.
7. Carpenter, ed., *The Letters*, 111.
8. Tolkien, *The Lord of the Rings*, 962.
9. Ibid., 950.
10. Carpenter, ed., *The Letters*, 252.
11. Tolkien, *Tree and Leaf*, 68–69.
12. Tolkien, *The Lord of the Rings*, 255–56.
13. Carpenter, ed., *The Letters*, 253.
14. Ibid., 69.
15. Lewis, *The Chronicles of Narnia*, 185.
16. Ibid., 737.
17. Ibid., 759.
18. In his essay "On Fairy-Stories," Tolkien leaves no doubt about his understanding of the central meaning of Christianity. "The Birth of Christ is the eucatastrophe of Man's history. The Resurrection is the eucatastrophe of the story of the Incarnation. This story begins and ends in joy." Tolkien, *Tree and Leaf*, 72.
19. Isaacs and Zimbardo, eds., *Tolkien and the Critics*, 248.
20. Tolkien, *Tree and Leaf*, 69.
21. Tolkien, *The Lord of the Rings*, 954.
22. Ezra 3:11–12.
23. Churchill, *The World Crisis*, 3–4.
24. Meyer, *World Undone*, 260.

25. Quoted in Dan Rodricks, "The Sad, Senseless End of Henry Gunther," *Baltimore Sun*, November 11, 2008, http://articles.baltimoresun.com/2008–11–11 /news/0811100097_1_henry-gunther-11th-month-war-i.

26. Overy, *The Twilight Years*, 12.

27. T. S. Eliot, *The Wasteland and Other Poems* (Orlando: Harcourt Brace & Company), 33.

28. Remarque, *All Quiet on the Western Front*, 294.

29. Lewis, *The Chronicles of Narnia*, 339.

30. Ibid., 766.

31. MacDonald, *Phantastes*, 188.

32. C. S. Lewis, ed., *George MacDonald: An Anthology* (New York: HarperCollins, 2001), xxxv.

33. Lewis, *The Chronicles of Narnia*, 557–558.

34. Lewis, ed., *George MacDonald*, xxxv.

35. Tolkien, *The Lord of the Rings*, 968.

36. Joel 3:14.

37. Tolkien, *The Lord of the Rings*, 953.

38. Revelation 22:5.

A Remembrance

1. *The Story of the 91st Division* (San Francisco: H.S. Crocker Co., Inc., 1919), 19.

2. Ibid., 32.

INDEX

ABOUT THE AUTHOR

J oseph Loconte is an Associate Professor of History at the King's College in New York City, where he teaches courses on Western Civilization and American Foreign Policy. His commentary on international human rights and religious freedom has appeared in the nation's leading media outlets, including the *New York Times*, the *Wall Street Journal*, the *Washington Post*, the *New Republic*, the *Weekly Standard*, and National Public Radio. He is a regular contributor to the *Huffington Post* and the London-based *Standpoint* magazine. He serves as a senior fellow at the Trinity Forum and as an affiliated scholar at the John Jay Institute. A native of Brooklyn, New York, he divides his time between New York City and Washington DC.